Magic Mirror

Download Companion Resources at
magicmirrorbook.com

Also by Meagan Pollock

Together, We Can Make The World Better
Children's Book with Discussion Guide

Quotes and Questions for Reflection and Dialogue
Prompts for Meaningful Conversation-Starters
and Reflective Journaling

Magic Mirror Workbook
A Reflective Journey through the
Positionality Prism's Nine Practices

Magic Mirror

Nine Practices to Be a Better
Leader, Colleague, Educator,
Neighbor, Friend, and More

MEAGAN POLLOCK, PHD

Copyright 2025 by Meagan Pollock.

All rights reserved.

Intentionally Engineer Inclusion® is a registered trademark owned by Meagan Pollock.

No part of this publication may be reproduced, distributed, or transmitted in any form or by any means, including photocopying, recording, or other electronic or mechanical methods, without the prior written permission of the publisher, except in the case of brief quotations embodied in critical reviews and certain other noncommercial uses permitted by copyright law. For more details, please refer to the Materials Use Policy at https://drmp.co/policy. For permission requests, please contact the author at info@meaganpollock.com.

This book may be purchased in bulk for business or educational use.

Dr. Meagan Pollock is available for virtual and in-person keynote talks, seminars, panels, and workshops on the concepts in this book and beyond. She brings expertise on a range of related topics to meet the unique needs of audiences and organizations.

Library of Congress Control Number: 2025900193

ISBN: 978-1-7324678-2-8 (hardback)

ISBN: 978-1-7324678-3-5 (paperback)

ISBN: 978-1-7324678-4-2 (e-book)

How to Cite This Book: Pollock, M. (2025). Magic Mirror: Nine Practices To Be A Better Leader, Colleague, Educator, Neighbor, Friend, and More. 7E Ventures Press.

The web addresses referenced in this book were live and correct at the time of the book's publication but may be subject to change.

This book is a work of fiction intended to provide insights and reflections for personal and professional development. Some stories are amalgamations or extensions of real-world experiences, while names, characters, places, and incidents are either the product of the author's imagination or are used fictitiously. Any resemblance to actual events, locales, or persons, living or dead, is entirely coincidental.

Cover design, graphics, and book layout by Meagan Pollock.

FIRST EDITION: JANUARY 2025

For additional resources and updates, visit: magicmirrorbook.com

FOR MY PARENTS,
PHIL AND DEANNE

CONTENTS

Preface	xi
Ask The Question	1
Search for Answers	5
Meet the Mentor	11
Reveal the Path	16

Positionality Prism Part 1: Personhood

Explore Your Identity — Lesson **25**
*Unpack who you are and see how
your identity shapes your world.* — Reflection **38**

Assess Salient Roles — Lesson **43**
*Discover which parts of your identity take
center stage in various situations and why.* — Reflection **50**

Identify Bridges & Barriers — Lesson **54**
*Pinpoint aspects of your identity that help
or hinder your journey and relationships.* — Reflection **64**

Positionality Prism Part 2: Perception

Check Your Filter
LESSON **71**
Reflect on how your experiences shape quick judgments and actions.
REFLECTION **84**

Expand Your Perspective
LESSON **88**
Challenge assumptions and ask, "What else might be true?" to build empathy.
REFLECTION **98**

See Beyond Yourself
LESSON **106**
Understand others' behaviors by recognizing their unique struggles and experiences.
REFLECTION **112**

Positionality Prism Part 3: Power

Recognize Your Power
LESSON **119**
Reflect on your advantages, influence, and resources—and how they shape your life.
REFLECTION **126**

Share Power
LESSON **131**
Step back, make space, and create opportunities for others to thrive.
REFLECTION **137**

Disrupt Barriers
LESSON **145**
Examine the structures that limit progress and find ways to challenge and reshape them.
REFLECTION **159**

Moving Forward

Reflect on the Journey
167

Spread the Word
172

A Note From The Author
176

Appendix

Mira's Social Identity Map — 183

Summary: 9 Positionality Practices — 184

Reflection and Discussion Guide — 186

Key Terms — 189

Endnotes & Additional Reading — 200

Acknowledgments — 202

About the Author — 206

Preface

Stories have the unique power to teach, connect, and help us see the world in new ways. *Magic Mirror* is one such story—a modern fable that explores how our identities and experiences shape our understanding and actions.

I wrote this book because studying and practicing **positionality** transformed how I see and engage in the world. I began recognizing how my background, assumptions, and experiences expanded and limited my perspective. This journey has helped me strive toward greater empathy and alignment with the person I want to be. While I continue to learn and grow on this journey, I believe in sharing the research and approach I teach to help others. Through storytelling, I aim to make these complex ideas accessible, revealing truths that can often feel elusive in theoretical discussions.

If the term positionality is new to you, don't worry—this story will guide you step by step, gradually uncovering its meaning and showing its impact through lessons and reflections.

Book Structure

This book is structured around the **Positionality Prism** framework, divided into three sections that explore Personhood, Perception, and Power. Each section contains three lessons, introducing nine practices in total. After each lesson with Elara, the guide, the protagonist, Mira, reflects on how to bridge the gap between theory and practice.

Engaging with This Book

Here are a few recommendations for engaging with this book and getting the most out of its lessons.

- **Solo Reading**: Start by reading the book all the way through for a complete understanding. Then, revisit it one practice at a time. Access the companion workbook or sign up for a course to assist you in reflecting and applying the lessons.
- **Book Club or Team Reads**: Share the experience with others. Discuss the lessons to deepen understanding and inspire meaningful dialogue. A discussion guide is in the appendix, or you can download expanded versions customized for various audiences at magicmirrorbook.com.
- **Organizational Training**: Use the book to spark growth and transformation in your workplace or community. Consider inviting me to lead a workshop, seminar, or keynote speech.

Resources to Support Your Journey

- **Glossary**: Key terms are boldly highlighted, generally at first mention, and defined in the appendix.
- **Reflection & Discussion Guide**: Found at the end of the book and online to support both individual and group learning.
- **Summary of Practices**: A quick reference guide to the nine practices is included in the appendix.

- **Additional Resources**: Visit my website at magicmirrorbook.com for free downloads, journaling guides, and tools to support your learning. New resources may be added.

As you read, I hope *Magic Mirror* will challenge you to reflect deeply, connect authentically, and act courageously. Together, we can create a ripple effect of positive change across our lives, workplaces, classrooms, and communities.

Meagan Pollock, PhD

Download Your Free Companion Workbook and Access Exclusive Resources

Scan the QR code or visit
magicmirrorbook.com
to access tools designed to help you reflect, apply the lessons, and take meaningful action.

CHAPTER 1

Ask The Question

The café was bustling, a low hum of conversation blending with the clatter of cups and plates and the soft strains of instrumental music playing from the speakers. Mira's favorite corner table—their table—felt like a refuge, but not today. Today, it seemed to trap her under the weight of her own emotions. Mira didn't understand why she was crying. The café was their sanctuary, a space where she and Ruby had shared countless conversations and laughter. She had always prided herself on keeping her emotions in check, especially in public. But now, here she was, sitting across from her best friend Ruby, tears softly falling down her cheeks.

Mira glanced at the sunlight streaming through the café's tall windows, hoping to ground herself, to shake off whatever was unraveling inside her. She tried to brush the tears away with her sleeve, hoping no one around them noticed, but they wouldn't stop. Ruby's story wasn't even the worst thing she'd heard. It was more about how it made her feel about herself that broke her. A deep, nagging fear that maybe, just maybe, she wasn't the friend she thought she was.

Ruby looked tired, her voice wavering as she described her struggles at work. The usual warmth in her tone was replaced by a weariness that Mira couldn't ignore. As Ruby detailed the subtle insults and the constant undermining remarks she endured daily, Mira felt a pang of helplessness—an unshakable sense that her silence was failing her friend. She listened, nodding when it felt appropriate, but her words seemed lodged somewhere unreachable. Ruby sighed, her voice trailing off, and Mira's heart sank at the unspoken distance forming between them. Ruby glanced at Mira, noticing the tears streaking her cheeks. For a brief moment, annoyance flickered in her eyes as though she realized the tears weren't entirely for her story but for Mira's own discomfort. She didn't say anything, but the pause lingered, heavy with unsaid words. When Ruby changed the subject, Mira let her, unsure of what to say, the weight of inadequacy settling in. In that sigh, Mira felt a quiet disappointment—not just in the world, but perhaps in herself, too.

Later that day, Mira was walking her rescue dog, Molly, around the neighborhood. The sun was bright, and the sky was almost offensively clear, given how she felt inside. As they made their way along the sidewalk in front of the new homes, a group of kids approached with fishing poles, hopeful expressions lighting up their faces. Mira knew what was coming. "Miss, can we fish in your backyard today?" one of the boys asked, nodding toward her property, which backed up to a beautiful, sprawling spring-fed lake.

She hesitated before answering, her throat tightening. "Not today, boys. Sorry," she said, almost wincing at her own words. The kids frowned, turned, and one boy muttered under his breath, "We got to fish here all the time until your dumb houses were built." Mira swallowed hard, their words echoing in her head. *Until your dumb houses were built.* She watched them walk away, a hollow feeling blooming in her chest. She used to let them fish, but over time, the stories about liability and her neighbors' warnings about safety had worn her down. She wasn't proud of it. She could feel herself making excuses, and none of them felt right.

That evening, Mira attended an outreach event for a local nature-based STEM (Science, Technology, Engineering, and Math) initiative aimed at kids in urban areas. She volunteered often, and she normally enjoyed it. Today, though, the words from her fellow volunteers grated on her. "These kids need us to bring nature to them," one volunteer said, smiling as she handed a child a test tube for a water quality experiment. "Without us, they'd never have the opportunity to understand this stuff." Mira smiled politely, but the phrasing made her stomach turn. *These kids. Us.* It was subtle, but it carried a subtext she couldn't ignore—a line drawn that shouldn't be there. Again, she found herself saying nothing, the discomfort simmering beneath her polite expression.

As if the day hadn't been exhausting enough, that night, she opened her laptop to find a resignation email from one of her best employees, Brooke. The email was polite but direct—the employee had found a new job, one with a culture that better suited her growth. Mira could see it now: the times during their one-on-ones when Brooke had tried to communicate her struggles, and Mira had told her to "stay optimistic" that things would get better. Mira had thought she was being supportive. But maybe she had just been dismissive, trying to slap positivity on a deeper wound. The realization cut deep.

Mira curled up on her couch that night, Molly resting her head on her lap. She opened a book, but the words blurred together. Her mind raced, replaying the moments from the day—Ruby's sigh, the kids walking away, the comments at the STEM event, Brooke's polite resignation. Was she truly making a difference? Or was she just another well-meaning person inadvertently making things worse? She felt disconnected, not just from the people around her but from the version of herself she wanted to be.

She thought back to the events of the day, each moment leaving her feeling more disconnected and unsure. A single question rose above the rest, cutting through the noise in her mind: *What kind of person do I want to be?* The weight of this question settled over her, demanding attention. It wasn't new—it had lingered in the corners of her mind for months, maybe longer. But today, something shifted. Maybe it was the accumulation of everything, or maybe she was just tired of how things felt. Either way, she knew one thing: she couldn't keep ignoring this feeling. It was time to take action.

CHAPTER 2

Search for Answers

Mira felt fiercely determined. She wanted to be a better person—a better friend, a better neighbor, a better leader—someone who could show up meaningfully for the people she cared about. She wanted to truly understand others' lived experiences and find ways to bridge the gaps between them. She wanted to connect better with her colleagues, to understand the layers of her friendships, and ultimately to create environments where people felt they belonged. She knew she was ready for something beyond just theory—she needed tangible ways to bring empathy and understanding into her daily life, at home, and at work. She wanted to learn, grow, and change. *But how? How could she do this?*

An Internet search seemed like a reasonable place to start, so she prompted a search engine with the question, "How do I become a better person?" The AI overview summarized a helpful list:

- Take care of yourself: Get enough sleep, eat healthily, and exercise.

- Be honest: Don't lie, cheat, or fib to anyone.
- Let go of anger: Learning to manage and let go of anger can help you be your best self.
- Identify your values: Feel that you are living in alignment with your values.
- Enhance your strengths: People who use their strengths effectively report higher levels of well-being, motivation, and job satisfaction.
- Be helpful: Find small ways to be helpful in your daily interactions with others.
- Think before you speak: Consider your words before you say something or respond to others.
- Practice self-reflection: Try journaling and changing your perspective.
- Work on accountability: Practice forgiveness and try new things.
- Keep learning: Continue to learn and grow.

Mira skimmed the list. It seemed straightforward and not far off from what she already thought, though she wouldn't have guessed healthy eating and exercise as number one. *Note to self: eat broccoli and ride the stationary bike later*, she mused. Re-reading the list to see what her action plan might be, the last five tugged at her more insistently than the others. She wanted to be more helpful, thoughtful, self-aware, accountable, and a lifelong learner. But the same question remained—how? How could she do that?

As she scrolled through the search results, she saw a sponsored ad that read: "Magic Mirror: One look makes you a better person." Mira hesitated but clicked what she was sure would be clickbait, leading to some dark corner of the web destined to rob her of her identity. Instead, a bright and cheerfully colored page quickly loaded. A series of questions scrolled across the screen, each on a banner featuring a happy, smiling person. "Do you want to be a better person? Do you want to be an influential leader? Do you want to be a bold **ally**?"

"Yes, why yes, I do," she thought as if her computer screen was mysteriously channeling her innermost thoughts, hopes, and dreams.

As Mira scrolled through the website, the testimonials caught her eye.

Ana, Community Organizer: "Looking into the Magic Mirror was a life-changing experience. I thought I understood my role in the community, but I didn't realize how my own privileges sometimes kept me from truly seeing others. It opened my eyes to the subtle ways power and privilege operate in our everyday interactions, helping me see my community in a new light. I left more committed than ever to using my position to uplift those around me. I wasn't sure what to expect, but something in that experience changed me completely."

Thomas, School Principal: "The Magic Mirror helped me understand what it means to lead with empathy. The experience helped me see the impact of my decisions from new angles I had not considered before. It was humbling to realize how policies that seem neutral can actually perpetuate inequity. Now, I approach my role with a deeper awareness of who benefits and who might be left behind."

Jada, Small Business Owner: "I used to think that hard work was all it took to succeed, but the Magic Mirror showed me that the playing field isn't even for everyone. It made me reconsider the idea of success and think about how I can make my business more supportive for everyone."

Elias, Healthcare Worker: "Accessing the Magic Mirror was like holding a lens up to my own biases. Working in healthcare, I thought I was compassionate, but the experience taught me to be more aware of struggles I might have otherwise overlooked and helped me improve how I care for my patients."

Sophia, City Council Member: "The Magic Mirror revealed to me how my own privileges influenced the way I created and voted on policies. It reminded me of the importance of actively learning about others' barriers so I could better advocate for meaningful change. It wasn't what I imagined, but it left me transformed."

Ava, Team Manager: "As a manager, I prided myself on being fair and impartial. The Magic Mirror experience helped me see that fairness isn't just about treating everyone the same; it's about understanding what people need to thrive. It also helped me recognize and redirect aspects of our team culture that weren't as inclusive as I thought. Now, I'm fostering an environment where everyone feels valued and empowered to contribute their best, and if I am not, I've helped to create enough psychological safety so that people can speak up and let me know."

Liam, Team Member: "Using the Magic Mirror gave me insight into how my own actions and assumptions affect the people I work with every day. I didn't realize how small things—like who I choose to collaborate with or how I interpret others' ideas—could undermine a sense of belonging. It helped me become more intentional in building trust and creating a workplace where everyone feels they truly belong. I left feeling empowered to make a difference, even in the little things."

Mira frowned, intrigued but cautious. She didn't know much about privilege, bias, or inequity, and thanks to the zeitgeist, she was a little bit wary of the concepts. But as she kept reading, something began to shift inside her—an urgency, a hunger. It sounded too good to be true. She knew people sometimes exaggerated experiences online, but these words felt different. There was a sincerity in the way they described their transformations—like they had seen themselves, truly seen, for the first time. Mira found herself wondering whether she had ever really seen herself that way. What if the discomfort she felt now was exactly what she needed to truly grow? Mira bit her lip, a dubious chuckle escaping. "Sure, a magic mirror," she muttered, shaking her head. But the pull was there; beneath her skepticism was something deeper—a sense of hope she couldn't quite dismiss. What if there was more to this mirror than just an empty promise? What if she could finally find the answers she was searching for?

Mira found herself staring at the screen, her mind buzzing with possibilities. Could it be that simple? The people in the testimonials spoke with such clarity, convincing her that they had discovered something she couldn't quite grasp. For so long, she had felt stuck, watching herself make the same mistakes, feeling the strain of not knowing how to change. But here, just a click away, was something that might help her break free from the cycle of confusion. With a deep breath, she clicked on the contact page, half-worried it was all a scam, half-hoping it would be her turning point.

With a quick skim of the page, she found that the Magic Mirror was right here in her town, and she could schedule an appointment immediately.

Mira hovered over the appointment button, her heart racing. Was this a good idea? She had tried books, seminars, and even some half-hearted journaling, but nothing had ever stuck. This time felt different, even though the advertisement and website read exactly like a quick fix. However, she wasn't just looking for a quick fix—she wanted something that could actually help her change the way she connected with others, how she showed up at work, and how she understood herself. She needed more than theory—she needed real, practical change.

Her eyes drifted to the corner of her screen, where the photo of her with her team smiled back at her—an image from months ago before the resignation emails started coming. They looked happy then, hopeful, like they were all part of something meaningful. Mira wanted that feeling back—the confidence that she knew what she was doing, that she was the kind of person who made things better for the people around her. Before she could change her mind, she clicked 'Book Now,' her breath catching in her throat as the confirmation page loaded. Was she being impulsive? Maybe. But she also knew that change didn't happen by staying safe. Her hesitation was a product of her past, of the narratives she had built about needing to be careful, needing to prove herself. But maybe, just maybe, real growth meant being willing to take a leap—to stop hiding behind caution and actually confront the changes she needed. Something had to change, and this felt like a sign.

CHAPTER 3

Meet the Mentor

The next day, Mira set out for the address she had received after booking her appointment. To her surprise, it wasn't far—a little more than a twenty-minute drive from her home, hidden at the edge of a forest she'd driven past countless times but never noticed. There were no signs, no obvious markers—just a narrow path leading deeper into the woods. It seemed strange to her that something so potentially powerful could be so close, almost as if it had always been there, waiting for her to notice it. Was that part of the magic? Perhaps this location was just for her, and it would be just around the corner for everyone else, too?

As she walked along the winding path, Mira felt a growing sense of anticipation mixed with disbelief. The forest seemed to shift around her, the sunlight filtering through the leaves—creating patterns on the ground that looked almost like runes. Small aster wildflowers, native to the ecosystem, nestled in the grasses. Bees and butterflies flitted between the salvia and black-eyed Susans. As a Certified Master Naturalist, she was in her element. Mira wondered if the Magic Mirror presented the same to everyone or if it shifted to reflect something in her. Suddenly,

Mira startled herself with worry that she had taken a wrong turn when, a few steps ahead, the trees parted, and there it was.

A small, simple structure stood before her—a place that seemed both ordinary and extraordinary. Ivy twisted up the sides of a cottage, and flowers bloomed in abundance, their colors too vivid to be real. The air smelled of herbs, sweet florals, and something else, something indescribable—almost like the scent of possibility.

Mira approached the door, her heart pounding. The door opened with a slight creak as if it had been expecting her. She stepped inside, her eyes widening at what she saw. The room was filled with ancient symbols, both carved into the wooden beams and painted on the walls. An ambient glow suffused the space, though there seemed to be no clear source of light. It was peaceful yet charged with energy, as if every object was alive with purpose.

And in the center of the room stood the mirror.

It wasn't hidden or disguised—there was no velvet cloth draped over it, no locks or guards. It stood openly, its ornate golden frame carved with intricate symbols, glowing faintly as if it had always been there, available for anyone brave enough to look. The surface of the mirror rippled like water, almost as if it was inviting her to step closer.

Mira's pulse quickened. Was this it? The Magic Mirror. A mirror anyone could find, yet it radiated power she couldn't quite describe. She reached out, hesitating for just a moment as the surface shimmered, almost as if it was alive and waiting to see if she truly had the courage to touch it.

Just as her fingertips hovered inches away, a voice broke the stillness, rich and melodic yet commanding—a voice that seemed to echo both within her ears and somewhere deeper, as though the very air around her had spoken. It wasn't loud, but it carried a warmth and authority that made Mira freeze mid-motion.

"Hello, Mira, and welcome to the Magic Mirror sanctuary. I'm Elara, and I'll be your guide on this journey."

Mira turned, startled, and found herself face to face with a serene-looking woman whose eyes seemed to hold an ancient wisdom, like they had witnessed countless lifetimes. Her long, waist-length locks of greyish-white cascaded around her shoulders, shimmering faintly in the light like moonlit strands. Her skin, a deep, rich brown with undertones of warmth, seemed to absorb the glow of the room, enhancing her presence with a quiet radiance.

Elara's white, flowing outfit draped loosely over her frame, the fabric moving gently with each small motion as if catching an unseen breeze. Her sandals were simple but sturdy, their well-worn leather hinting at countless journeys. Despite her unassuming attire, she radiated an aura of quiet strength and timeless grace, as though she was both grounded in the present and intimately connected to something far greater.

Elara's magnificence triggered something in Mira, an insecurity that she couldn't explain. Looking at her questioningly, she responded almost petulantly, "What journey? I thought I just looked in the mirror, and all would be revealed to me!" Internally, Mira was conflicted. She had already been on a journey. She had been putting in the effort and came ready to learn more. But suddenly, the task seemed insurmountable, and she was filled with fear and trepidation about what the Magic Mirror would reveal.

Elara's face, illuminated brilliantly, cradled a growing and knowing smile. "It's not that simple, my dear. The mirror can show you the truth, but to truly understand and grow, you need to take a journey that will reveal who you are, the systems that shape you, and the world around you. You've come here for clarity, but clarity comes with courage."

Mira frowned, her curiosity warring with frustration, undergirded by her fears. "I just want to be better—more empathetic, a better leader, someone who can speak up and make a difference."

Elara nodded. "And you can. But understand this, Mira—this journey is not one you can turn back from. Once you see the world as it truly is, you can never unsee it. You can pause; you can take breaks. You may even feel overwhelmed at times. But there is always more to learn, more to understand. Growth is endless, and the mirror will be your companion if you are ready."

Mira swallowed hard, absorbing the gravity of Elara's words. "Are there risks?" she asked, her voice barely above a whisper.

Elara's gaze softened. "The risks are real. You may come to see parts of yourself that are difficult to accept. You may recognize advantages you've had that others haven't. It can be uncomfortable, even painful. But the reward is truth, the kind of truth that changes how you see the world—and how you can make it better. You have to be willing to face that, Mira."

Mira hesitated, her heart pounding. "What if I fail? What if I can't handle it?"

Elara smiled gently. "Failure is part of the process, Mira. This is not about perfection; it's about learning, about being willing to continue even when it's hard. Some people pause forever, some never finish—but the journey itself is where the growth happens."

She extended her hand toward the mirror, and as she did, the golden frame shimmered, tiny sparks of light dancing along its edges. The room pulsed gently with energy as though it were alive, responding to Elara's intent. The mirror's surface rippled like liquid glass, reflecting not just Mira's face but glimmers of distant scenes and faint, shadowy figures.

"Are you ready to begin?" Elara asked, her voice steady but tinged with an almost mystical resonance. "This mirror will guide you to meet people who will reveal different facets of the truth—

realities of advantages, disadvantages, and the systems that shape us all. These are experiences you'll carry with you, illuminating your path and transforming how you see and act in the world."

Mira took a deep breath, her eyes shifting between Elara and the shimmering mirror. The uncertainty tugged at her, but the pull of something greater—a possibility of change, of real growth—felt stronger.

"I'm ready," Mira whispered, stepping toward the mirror.

Elara nodded. "Then let's begin."

CHAPTER 4

Reveal the Path

Mira sat cross-legged on a large, intricately patterned rug, her eyes on Elara, who stood before the glowing mirror. The room had an ancient but welcoming feel—filled with symbols and artifacts that seemed to vibrate with unspoken stories. Mira still couldn't quite believe she was here, in a room that seemed to exist between reality and a dream.

Elara smiled warmly, her eyes glinting with both kindness and a knowing seriousness. "Mira, the journey you're about to undertake isn't about answers. It's about exploration, reflection, and, most of all, growth. Today, I will introduce you to the roadmap that will guide you."

She pointed delicately, and the mirror quivered with energy. Its surface rippled, a soft glow expanding until it filled the entire room. Mira felt warmth from the glow, as if the room itself was readying for something extraordinary.

"Before we dive into the details, it's important to understand the concept that underpins this entire journey: positionality," Elara continued. "**Positionality** is about recognizing how your identity, experiences, and social context shape your perspective of the world. It influences how you relate to others, how you interpret situations, and, ultimately, how you choose to act. By understanding your own positionality, you begin to understand the lenses through which you view everything—yourself, others, and the world. This journey will be about examining and understanding your positionality—how your unique context frames your experiences and how adjusting that frame can lead to more meaningful connections and growth."

Elara paused for a moment, allowing the words to settle before continuing, "Your journey will center on three key themes: **Personhood**, **Perception**, and **Power**. These are not just abstract ideas; they are lenses through which we understand our identities, others, and our place in the world. Together, these themes form a prism. When illuminated by the light of awareness, the full spectrum of our identities and experiences is revealed. Yet awareness alone is not enough—it must inspire intentional action to reshape how we move through the world and connect with others. Each theme will guide a step in your journey, introducing **Positionality Practices**—ongoing habits that deepen your awareness and empower you to take meaningful action."

Mira nodded, absorbing Elara's words. It felt like she was being handed a map—not to a physical place but to a new understanding of herself and the world. She thought of her work, the people she struggled to connect with, and the times she felt like she was missing something vital. Maybe this journey was exactly what she needed to make those connections and build the relationships that seemed just out of reach.

Then, her brow furrowed slightly before her face lit up with a small smile chased by a chuckle. "Positionality Practices of Personhood, Perception, Power. Pieces that make a prism. I see what you did there! There's something *purposeful* about those P's, isn't there?"

Elara's lips curved into a knowing smile. "It's no accident, Mira. The alliteration is a way to help you remember—but it's the depth behind the words that truly matters."

Mira laughed softly. "Well, I guess I'm ready to unlock their purpose."

"Let's begin with **Personhood**," Elara said, her voice gentle but firm.

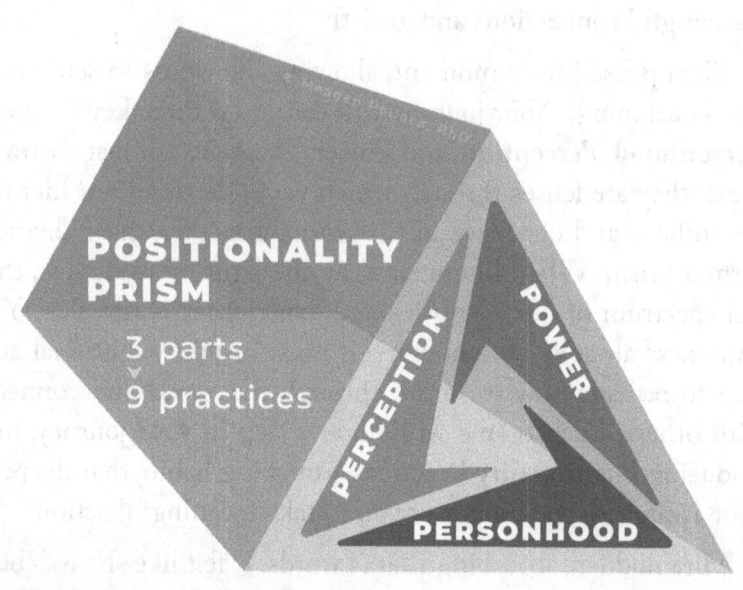

"**Personhood is the foundation.** It involves understanding who you are—acknowledging the layers that make up your identity, your values, and the roles you inhabit. Every one of us carries experiences that influence how we see the world—our culture, our background, the privileges we hold, and the barriers we face. These layers form the lens through which we experience everything, and understanding them is the first step to truly understanding the impact we have on others. You must start by examining yourself and the different facets of your life that influence your choices. We often overlook how deeply interconnected these layers are, but understanding them will help you recognize how you see the world."

She paused and walked toward Mira, handing her a small journal with a soft leather cover with *Mira* embossed in sweeping cursive gold letters that shimmered in the light reflected by the mirror. "Take this. This will be your companion throughout the journey. I want you to use it to record your reflections, your realizations, and the questions that come up along the way. The more honest you are with yourself, the more transformative this experience will be."

Elara gestured toward the mirror once more, and as if in response, the surface rippled like a pond disturbed by a single drop of water. Gradually, the shimmer resolved into vivid scenes, each alive with movement and emotion. Mira leaned in, her breath catching as the images unfolded before her.

She saw a young boy in a bustling city, clutching a tattered backpack as he dashed through the rain. The determination in his eyes was palpable. The scene shifted to a woman standing at a podium, her voice confident as she spoke to a crowded room. Mira could almost hear the faint echo of her words, resonating with courage. Another ripple revealed an elderly man sitting alone in a sunlit room, his hands trembling as he held a faded photograph.

Each glimpse was layered with complexity—moments of joy, pain, triumph, and struggle. Mira could feel the weight of their emotions as if the mirror wasn't just showing her their lives but inviting her to step into them. The connection was visceral; it made her heart ache and soar simultaneously.

The mirror pulsed gently, and Mira realized it wasn't just a window to these lives—it was a bridge, a way to see the humanity and depth in each experience. Her fingertips tingled with anticipation, and for the first time, she fully understood the enormity of what lay ahead.

"Next, we move to **Perception**," Elara said, her gaze fixed on the mirror as the scenes shifted. "Perception is about recognizing how your identity influences your view of the world and shapes your interpretations of others. It is about understanding how you are perceived by those around you—recognizing that their perceptions may be colored by their own stereotypes, biases, or past experiences that have nothing to do with you personally. It's the art of both seeing clearly and being seen clearly and understanding the barriers that can get in the way of that. The world is made of billions of perspectives, each shaped by unique experiences. To truly understand others, you must first understand how your own lens shapes what you see and, at times, frames your interpretation of the world. Recognizing this helps us see the richness of other people's experiences and be open to different perspectives."

Mira's heart pounded as she watched the scenes dance across the mirror. She understood, at least in theory, the need to step outside her own experiences. But she also knew that practice was much harder.

Elara turned to Mira. "Finally, there is **Power**. This is the theme that will challenge you the most. You will learn to identify the power you hold—whether it comes from your position, your privilege, or your experience—and how to use that power purposefully. You must recognize that with power comes responsibility. You have the opportunity to create change, but only if you first understand your position within the system."

Elara's eyes softened. "This journey is not linear. You will circle back, revisit themes, and find new insights as you grow. It will challenge you, but it will also open you up in ways you cannot yet imagine. Are you ready, Mira?"

Mira took a deep breath, looking at the glowing mirror. She felt something shift within her—a sense of readiness mixed with fear. "I think so," she whispered.

Elara smiled. "Good. Take a deep breath, Mira. This is the first step of a journey that will challenge and transform you." Mira placed her hand on the mirror's surface, and a warm light enveloped the room.

POSITIONALITY PRISM PART 1
Personhood

CHAPTER 5

Explore Your Identity
ELARA'S LESSON

The light from the mirror slowly dimmed, leaving Mira standing in front of a large wooden table in a new space. It looked like a library, with bookshelves lining the walls and sunlight streaming through tall windows. Elara stood by the table, a map laid out in front of her, covered with symbols and names Mira did not recognize.

"This," Elara said, "is where we begin our work on **Personhood**—the foundational piece of the Positionality Prism. Today, you will start creating your **Social Identity Map**[1]."

Mira looked at the map, confusion and curiosity warring in her mind. "What is a social identity map?" she asked, stepping closer.

Elara smiled, her expression warm but purposeful. "It is a way of exploring the different facets of your identity—how society defines you and how these identities influence your opportunities, your beliefs, and how you interpret the world around you." She gestured toward an empty parchment, and as she did, a soft golden glow traced the edges of the page as though awakening to her touch. Handing Mira a quill that shimmered faintly with an iridescent sheen, she added, "You will reflect on aspects of yourself—race, ethnicity, gender, socioeconomic status, ability status, and others. These identities are layered, and each carries different weights and impacts in different contexts."

Elara pointed to the parchment, and Mira watched in awe as faint lines and shapes emerged, forming the beginnings of a chart divided into three tiers. The chart seemed to hum with energy, its glow inviting her to engage. "This is your map," Elara said softly, her voice steady and encouraging. "A guide to understanding the layers of who you are."

The parchment shimmered, and words began to form as if ink were being drawn invisibly across its surface. Mira leaned closer, captivated by the unfolding message.

The parchment's text pulsed gently, emphasizing its importance. Mira read aloud, her voice hesitant but clear. "Tier 1: Social Identity. You will start by identifying the broader aspects of who you are—such as race, gender, and socioeconomic background. You will do this for multiple identities."

She glanced at Elara, who nodded in quiet affirmation. The parchment continued, almost as if it sensed her curiosity.

"Next is Tier 2: Life Impact." Mira read softly, "You will reflect on the impact of each identity. What opportunities or barriers has it created for you? What values have been tied to these identities? Consider how these facets influence how you interpret events."

As she spoke, the mirror shimmered, and images appeared within its surface—a young girl standing before a closed door, a hand extended in an offer of friendship, a storm of whispers in the background. Each scene seemed to resonate with the words Mira read, reflecting the layers of meaning in the instructions back to her.

Explore Your Identity | LESSON

The final tier revealed itself with a subtle shift in the parchment's light. Mira hesitated, her voice catching. "Finally, Tier 3: Emotions. You will dig into the emotions attached to each of these impacts. How does each facet make you feel? Empowered? Anxious? Perhaps even indifferent? Our feelings often reveal deeper insights about our relationship with our own identity."

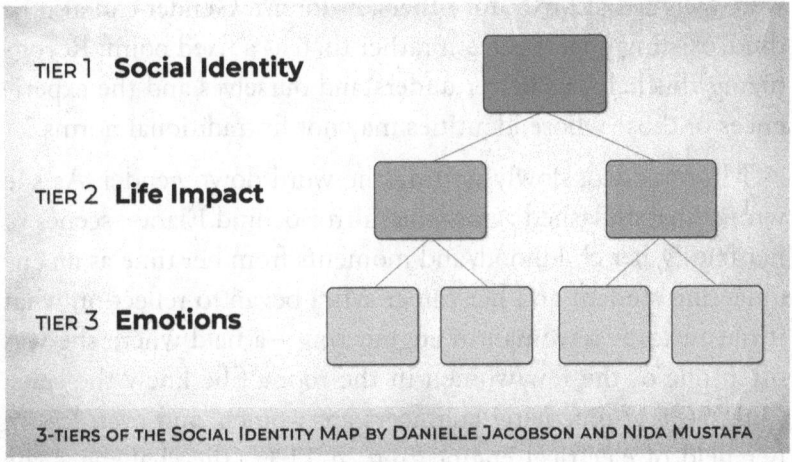

3-TIERS OF THE SOCIAL IDENTITY MAP BY DANIELLE JACOBSON AND NIDA MUSTAFA

The parchment's glow softened, giving Mira space to absorb its words. She stared at it, a swirl of emotions rising within her. It was daunting to think about her identities and even more so to explore how they interacted with the world. But in her mind, she thought about the moments when she struggled to connect with others—when she didn't understand what held her back. Maybe this map could help her navigate those uncertainties.

Mira turned to Elara, her voice small but determined. "I don't even know where to start."

Elara nodded, her voice tender. "That's alright, Mira. There is no right or wrong way to begin this. Let's take one aspect of your identity and go from there. How about we start with **gender** as your first Tier 1 to explore?"

She paused, her tone encouraging. "Gender is often misunderstood as being the same as **biological sex**, but they are distinct. Gender is about how you see and define yourself—your internal sense of identity—and how you choose to express it to the world. It's a **social construct**, meaning it's an idea created and accepted by society rather than something rooted in biology. Social constructs, like gender, are shaped by culture, history, and collective agreement. For some, gender aligns with the sex they were assigned at birth; for others, it doesn't. Gender can also be fluid, existing on a spectrum rather than as a fixed point. Recognizing this helps us better understand ourselves and the experiences of those whose identities may not fit traditional norms."

Mira nodded, slowly writing the word down gender. As she wrote, images flashed across the mirror behind Elara—scenes of her family, her childhood, and moments from her time as an engineering student and her career. Mira began to reflect on what it meant to be a woman in engineering—a field where she was often one of the few women in the room. She knew the stats: Only 16% of practicing engineers are women, and even less in her field of electrical engineering, at 11%.[2] The challenges she faced were not just personal struggles; they were reflections of broader societal dynamics. Her identity as a woman placed her in a position where she had to work against stereotypes, and those expectations influenced how she navigated every aspect of her career.

Elara walked over and stood beside her, watching the images unfold. "Gender can be a powerful aspect of identity," Elara said. "Think about your experiences in school and work—how did being a woman shape those experiences? This is the Tier 2, understanding the life impact."

Mira paused, her pen hovering above the parchment. "I remember university," she said slowly. "There were so few of us—women, I mean. I felt like I had to work twice as hard just to be taken seriously and to prove that I belonged there. It was exhausting, but it also pushed me to excel. I think, in a way, I internalized that pressure. I still carry it with me at work." Mira jotted some of these impacts for tier 2.

Elara nodded, ready to nudge Mira towards her tier 3 reflection of emotions attached to the life impacts of her gender. "That's a common experience. There is often pressure to overperform to break stereotypes, but that comes with a cost. How did that pressure make you feel?"

Mira thought for a moment before writing down words like *determined*, *isolated*, and *resentful*. "It made me proud of what I achieved," she said, "but also... I think I felt lonely. Like I couldn't show any weakness; it was like I had to constantly prove myself."

"And now?" Elara prompted. "Do you still feel that pressure?"

Mira sighed, nodding. "I do. Even now, as a practicing engineer and technical manager, I feel like I can't make mistakes. I have to always be on top of things and always be exceedingly competent. I guess it's this fear of confirming people's biases about women not being good at technical work."

Elara's eyes softened. "And how does that pressure influence your emotions and interactions today?"

Mira frowned as she wrote down more words: *stress, insecurity, pride*, and *resilience*. "It makes me careful but also anxious. I think it stops me from asking for help sometimes. I don't want to seem like I'm struggling, even when I am."

"That's important to recognize," Elara said gently. "These emotions are tied to how society sees gender—and how you have learned to navigate that as an engineer. It's a mix of resilience and the barriers that still exist. Understanding this helps you decide how to move forward—how to give yourself grace when needed, and how to acknowledge the challenges you face without internalizing them."

Mira nodded, her eyes misty. "I never really thought about it like that," she admitted. "I always just kept pushing forward."

"And that's admirable," Elara said. "But remember, understanding your identity isn't just about pushing forward. It's about understanding where you came from, the challenges you faced, and allowing yourself to grow through that understanding."

"Now, reflect on your race and your ethnicity," Elara encouraged, her tone inviting yet steady.

Mira hesitated, her pen hovering over the parchment. Finally, she admitted, "This is uncomfortable," her voice barely above a whisper. Her hand paused as she pushed the parchment slightly away, almost as if needing distance from the question.

Elara nodded, her expression kind and understanding. "It often is, Mira. Understanding ourselves at this level means confronting both the bridges and the barriers that shape our experiences. For many, this includes acknowledging benefits that might have come effortlessly, while others faced challenges you might have never seen. But this discomfort," she said gently, "is where growth begins. Why do you think it feels uncomfortable?"

Mira's eyes shifted downward, her voice tentative. "I guess I've never really thought about it or talked about this openly. I feel sort of conditioned to not talk about it, and I certainly don't remember learning about it in school."

Elara tilted her head thoughtfully. "Let's pause here for a moment and talk about what race and ethnicity mean—because this reflection isn't just about labels, but about understanding how these aspects of your identity have shaped your life."

She waved her fingers delicately, and the parchment shimmered faintly, floating gracefully back toward Mira. It landed softly in front of her as though nudging her to continue. Mira blinked, her initial discomfort momentarily replaced by a sense of curiosity at the subtle magic.

"**Race**," Elara explained, her tone calm and clear, "is a social construct—a category society created based on physical features like skin color or facial characteristics, such as being labeled as Black, White, or Asian. While it has no biological basis, it deeply shapes societal systems and influences how people are perceived and treated. **Ethnicity**, on the other hand, relates to shared cultural traits like language, traditions, or ancestry. For example, someone might identify as Hispanic, Jewish, or Han Chinese. While race is often imposed upon us by society, ethnicity tends to be something we claim for ourselves—a connection to the communities and histories we feel tied to."

The parchment seemed to faintly glow as though reflecting Mira's growing awareness. She glanced at Elara, her discomfort still present but softened by the sense of wonder surrounding her. "I never thought of it like that," she murmured, picking up her pen again.

"Often confused with ethnicity is **nationality**, which refers to a person's legal affiliation with a particular country, determined by birth, citizenship, or naturalization. Unlike race and ethnicity, nationality is tied to political boundaries and government recognition."

Mira reflected aloud to Elara, "Nationality seems simpler—for me, it's just American since I was born in the United States, right? But then again, it's not so simple for everyone. For me, it feels straightforward, but for others, like immigrants or people with dual citizenship, it's a lot more layered.

Mira picked up her pen and scribbled in the margin: *'Race = how others see me, Ethnicity = how I see myself?'* She paused, thinking aloud. "So... when someone asks me my race, they're probably assuming I'm White because of how I look. But my ethnicity? That's where my mom's Mexican heritage comes in—where I'm supposed to check 'Hispanic' on forms." She hesitated for a moment, tapping the pen against her chin.

Elara nodded, smiling gently. "That's right. In the United States, 'Hispanic' is a term often used to describe people with cultural ties to Spanish-speaking countries, especially in Latin America. But, like all labels, it doesn't fully capture the richness or complexity of individual identities. For example, your mom's connection to Mexico is part of your ethnicity, but your racial identity may be perceived differently, depending on the context or who's looking at you."

Mira leaned back slightly, processing this. "That makes sense. I guess I've always felt... torn. At school, I didn't want to stand out, so I leaned into the 'White' part of me because it was easier to fit in. I even remember feeling embarrassed when my mom spoke Spanish in front of my friends."

Elara's expression softened as she leaned forward, prompting Mira to move to Tier 2 of her reflections about the impact of the identity on her life. "How do you think that choice to 'fit in' has shaped who you are today?"

Mira sighed, pausing for a moment before she picked up her pen and began to write on the parchment. The words came slowly but deliberately: *opportunity, acceptance, erasure*. She looked at what she had written, then spoke softly. "I think it gave me access—people accepted me more easily when I blended in. But it also meant pushing away a part of my heritage. I rarely speak Spanish anymore, and it feels like a loss. I guess I chose acceptance over authenticity."

Elara nodded thoughtfully. "Those words you've written—opportunity, acceptance, erasure—they hold so much meaning. They show how identities are often shaped by the systems and expectations around us. The **dominant culture** often tells us what's acceptable or easier to be, and adapting to those expectations can open some doors while closing others. And how does that make you feel? Let's move to Tier 3—exploring the emotions attached to these impacts."

Mira frowned, thinking hard before writing down: *regret, discomfort*, and *conflict*. "I feel regret, mostly. Like I lost something that I can't quite get back. And discomfort—because I still find myself doing it today. Trying to fit in instead of embracing who I really am. There's always this conflict inside me."

Elara leaned closer, her voice imbued with quiet resolve. "It's a hard truth to face, but it's also powerful. Acknowledging this conflict is the first step towards healing it. You don't have to reject parts of yourself anymore, Mira. Part of understanding **Personhood** is realizing that every aspect of your identity, whether embraced or hidden, contributes to who you are. You have the power to reconnect with what you've pushed away."

Mira swallowed, nodding. "I think I want that. I want to reconnect."

"And you can," Elara said with a small, encouraging smile. "This journey is about embracing every facet of yourself—the parts that were celebrated and the parts that were hidden. Bringing all of who you are into the light is crucial for your growth."

Elara paused before continuing, her tone filled with measured patience. "All these aspects of your identity shape how you move through the world, whether you acknowledge them or not. Understanding Personhood means realizing that none of these facets exist in isolation. They are deeply interconnected and influenced by the social and political contexts around you, and those connections shape your experiences and interactions."

Mira nodded, feeling a mix of discomfort and revelation. Elara guided Mira to reflect on her **ability** next. "Tell me about your experiences related to ability. What do you notice when you think about how ability impacts your life?" she asked.

Mira paused, then began to write. "Physically, I appear able, but I have hidden disabilities. I live with narcolepsy, depression, and an old back injury. The narcolepsy means I have to plan my day meticulously to manage fatigue, and there's always the fear of suddenly dozing off during meetings." She sighed, writing more as images from her life flashed across the mirror. "The depression... it comes and goes, but sometimes it feels like a heavy cloud, making everything harder." She continued, noting how the back injury was due to overuse from 18 years of competing in powerlifting. Multiple failed surgeries, including a fusion, had left her in pain daily. She lives with that pain until she is ready to attempt another fusion. "People don't see these things," she sighed, "and that invisibility can make it feel even lonelier."

"How does all of this impact you in your work and personal life?" Elara asked, pointing towards Tier 2 of the chart.

Mira frowned, considering her response. "It makes me hesitant. Sometimes I avoid opportunities because I'm worried about my limitations. I think it affects how willing I am to advocate for myself. I also feel like I always have to compensate—if I'm tired or struggling, I don't want anyone to see it. It makes me feel..." She paused and began to write down words: *vulnerable, frustrated, resolute*.

"Now, let's explore those emotions," Elara said softly. "What do those feelings tell you about your experience of ability?"

Mira took a deep breath and wrote down *exhaustion, fear, resilience*, and *growth*. "I think there's a lot of fear there. Fear of being judged, of not being enough. But there's also resilience. I've learned to work with my limitations, to adapt, and keep going. In some ways, these challenges have also brought unexpected growth. I've developed empathy for others who struggle, and I've learned creative ways to solve problems that I might have overlooked if everything had been easy for me. The strength I've built has given me a unique perspective, and that's something I'm proud of."

Elara nodded, her expression compassionate. "It's important to recognize both—the challenges and the strengths you've developed because of them. Now, let's move to **socioeconomic status**, sometimes referred to as **social class**."

With a graceful sweep of her hand, a faint shimmer danced over the parchment, and a new heading appeared, illuminated briefly before settling into place. "**Socioeconomic status** refers to a combination of factors like income, education, and occupation, which together influence a person's access to resources and opportunities," she explained. "Social class, on the other hand, is a broader term that encompasses the societal hierarchies and divisions based on these factors, along with cultural and social norms. While socioeconomic status tends to be measured more tangibly—like wealth or job type—**social class** often reflects more intangible elements, such as the prestige or privilege associated with certain lifestyles or backgrounds."

Mira shifted in her seat, watching the parchment as if it was absorbing her thoughts. "I was raised middle class. My dad worked, and my mom stayed home. We lived in a small town, maybe 15,000 people. I went to public school, and I don't know if my parents struggled financially, but I do know there were things I wanted to do or participate in that were sometimes not in the family budget. I know this crushed my parents." She paused, writing down these reflections. "I went to a public university on scholarships, and I know that my college choice was limited to where I received scholarships, and the drive to earn money for college was seeded in me in first grade. This changed my approach to school and life for sure."

Elara nodded thoughtfully, extending her palm toward the parchment. The words Mira had written rearranged slightly, highlighting key phrases like "middle class," "scholarships," and "values." A soft, golden glow lingered briefly over Tier 2, drawing Mira's eyes to it.

"What impact do you think that had on your values and experiences?" Elara asked, her voice steady and inviting. The parchment shimmered gently again as if urging Mira to delve deeper into her reflections.

Mira thought for a moment. "I think it made me value hard work and independence. But it also made me feel like I was always trying to catch up, like I wasn't starting from the same place as some of my peers. I felt pressure to succeed so that the sacrifices my family made were worth it." She wrote down words like *independence, pressure, gratitude,* and *insecurity*.

"And how do those experiences shape your feelings today?" Elara asked.

Mira frowned, writing down her thoughts. "I feel *proud* but also *anxious*. I feel like I must always prove that I belong. There's always this background fear of not measuring up."

Elara smiled gently. "These experiences have shaped your journey, Mira. They are not just about what happened to you but about how you've carried those experiences into the present. This is part of understanding your **Personhood**—seeing how your past shapes your present emotions, behaviors, and values."

Mira nodded, feeling a deeper connection to the complexity of her own identity.

When they finally finished, Elara pointed to Mira's journal. "This is your take-home assignment, Mira. I want you to continue reflecting on this map, adding to it as new thoughts come to you. Explore how each facet influences not just your opportunities but also your emotions. And consider other parts of your identity—your age, citizenship, sexuality, religious beliefs, marital status, education, political ideology, appearance, or even your geographic location —and how they shape you. We are complex, and that complexity deserves to be understood."

Mira looked down at her map, then back at Elara. "I think I'm beginning to understand," she said softly.

Elara smiled. "That's all you need for now. Understanding will grow, just like you. The journey has just begun. I invite you to return next week for the next step. We will explore how different aspects of your identity become more or less important depending on the context you are in. The Magic Mirror sanctuary is a place of safety and protection, free of judgment and filled with understanding—a space where you can reflect, explore your positionality, and embrace your feelings without fear."

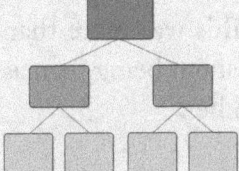

See part of Mira's Social Identity Map in the Appendix

CHAPTER 6

Explore Your Identity
MIRA'S REFLECTION

Mira sat in her small kitchen, the morning light filtering through the curtains, illuminating her journal spread out on the table before her. She absentmindedly traced her finger along the edges of the pages, her mind replaying her conversation with Elara from the day before. It was a lot to take in—the exploration of her gender, ethnicity, hidden disabilities, and socio-economic background. Each of these facets was like a puzzle piece, part of a larger picture of who she was.

Folded inside her journal was the parchment with the social identity map she had started. As she opened it up on the table, her eyes scanned the words she had written. Mira wanted to look at them with fresh eyes, beyond the labels she had initially assigned, and think deeper about how they shaped her current reality. There was no denying the truth in those words, but seeing them on paper made them feel more real, more impactful. Mira thought back to university, to the pressures of being one of the few women in her engineering classes. This was more than just about perfection—it was about survival, about being seen as equally capable in a space that often doubted her.

Reflecting on her gender was only one part of it. Mira also needed to unpack the pieces of her identity she had hidden—like her Mexican or Hispanic heritage. She had distanced herself from her family's culture, particularly the language, to fit in with her peers. This choice, she realized, was deeply rooted in her positionality as someone who had the privilege of blending into the dominant culture when it suited her—an option that others, who looked more visibly Hispanic, might not have had. It was a privilege that came with a cost—a choice she made for acceptance, but one that led to an erasure of an important part of herself. She remembered times in her youth when she deliberately avoided speaking Spanish, feeling it alienated her from her peers, often leading to awkward looks and questions. The regret sank deeper, a recognition of what she had lost while striving for acceptance. She remembered her mother, her affable voice speaking in Spanish as she cooked, the way Mira had brushed it off in her teenage years, refusing to engage in her mother's native language.

But it wasn't only about not fitting in with the dominant culture; Mira had also struggled to fit in with the Hispanic community. She often felt like an outsider there as well—too disconnected from her heritage, her language too rusty, her understanding of cultural nuances not deep enough. She remembered family gatherings where she felt lost, not quite belonging in either world. This feeling was exacerbated by her teasing uncles who relentlessly called only her, güera, slang for a girl or woman with lighter skin tones. The feeling of being "not enough" in either space had left her floating between identities, unsure of where she truly fit. The cost of trying to blend in had not just been the loss of authenticity with others but also a fragmented sense of self. She had been left without a community where she felt wholly understood, and that void weighed heavily on her. This struggle had impacted her relationships, her sense of belonging, and even how she viewed herself.

"I chose acceptance over authenticity," she whispered to herself, her pen hovering over her journal. Writing those words felt both painful and liberating. For the first time, she allowed herself to feel the regret that came from trying so hard to fit into the dominant culture—something that had seemed easier at the time but had left her feeling disconnected from her own roots.

She turned the page, her focus shifting to the hidden aspects of her ability status—her narcolepsy, her battle with depression, and the back injury from years of powerlifting. The images flashed in her mind: the long days managing fatigue, falling asleep in meetings, and facing judgment from colleagues who were unaware of her condition, assuming she was simply irresponsible. The times she fell behind on work buried under the heavy cloak of depression that sometimes burdened her. The pain that lingered in her back was a constant reminder of surgeries that had failed to bring relief. She wrote down three words: *frustration, resilience, and loneliness.*

The frustration stemmed from the unpredictability of her narcolepsy—those days when her body simply refused to cooperate. Resilience was what she had been forced to build, adapting her lifestyle, work schedule, and goals around her conditions. And loneliness—always present—was amplified by the invisibility of her disabilities. It was exhausting to live with conditions that others couldn't see, to always feel the need to be strong, to overcompensate for her challenges so that no one else would notice.

And yet, as she wrote, she realized something else—she had always found a way to adapt, to move forward. There was a strength in that, too. *"I've learned to work with my limitations,"* she wrote, her pen moving more confidently now. *"I've learned how to adapt, how to keep going even when it's hard."*

She looked over her map, noting the layers of her identity, and paused at the section on socioeconomic status. Growing up in a middle-class family, Mira recognized that financial limitations shaped many of her early experiences. She remembered times when certain activities or opportunities were out of reach because they simply weren't in the budget. This instilled in her a sense of gratitude for what she did have, as well as pressure to make the most out of every opportunity. She had carried this drive forward, determined to prove herself and to make her family's sacrifices worthwhile. It had become both a motivating force and a source of ongoing anxiety.

Mira set down her pen and took a deep breath, her eyes drifting to the window. The world outside moved steadily—people walked down the street, and cars passed by. She thought about Elara's words: Personhood is about how all these parts of yourself—visible and hidden—interconnect, shaping your choices, your worldview, and how you interact with others.

Mira wondered how these realizations would affect her as a leader, a neighbor, and a friend. How much of her inability to empathize had been rooted in her own efforts to fit in, to push aside parts of herself? If she couldn't be open about her own identity, how could she truly understand and support someone else's? How did her need to fit in and hide parts of herself impact her ability to genuinely connect with her team? She often encouraged openness and authenticity in others, but had she been doing the same herself? She knew now that the next step in her journey was not only about understanding herself but also about applying this understanding to her personal and professional goals.

She thought of the kids who had wanted to fish in her backyard—how she had hesitated, concerned about liability but also influenced by what her neighbors thought. Was her reaction another way of fitting into expectations rather than embracing her own values of connection and generosity? Was she unknowingly setting a standard that made others feel they needed to hide parts of who they were? These thoughts made her uneasy, but they also lit a spark of curiosity—what would it mean to lead with her whole self? To create a space where everyone felt they could do the same?

She realized that if she wanted others to feel truly seen and understood, she must first be willing to do that work herself. She needed to understand not only her visible strengths and vulnerabilities but also the privileges she carried, the biases she hadn't previously confronted, and how these shaped her leadership. It wasn't enough to expect openness from her team if she wasn't willing to model that same transparency, to acknowledge the ways her own experience as a White, educated professional had influenced her expectations and interactions. The journey ahead was going to be about more than understanding herself; it was about transforming how she led others.

She picked up her pen again, writing a note to herself: *"What else might I be missing when I listen to others? How can I be more aware of my lens and the biases it brings into what I hear?"*

This was her work now—to reflect, to understand, and to grow. She knew it wouldn't be easy. There were parts of this journey that would be uncomfortable, but she also knew that comfort wasn't the goal. Growth was. And growth meant challenging herself to see more clearly, to connect more deeply, and to embrace every part of herself.

Mira closed her journal and leaned back in her chair, feeling both exhausted and hopeful. She knew she had a long way to go, but for the first time, she felt like she was on the right path. Next week, she would return to Elara, ready to continue unraveling the complex layers of who she was.

"One step at a time," she whispered, a small smile tugging at her lips. "One step at a time."

CHAPTER 7

Assess Salient Roles
ELARA'S LESSON

Mira returned to the sanctuary the following week, her thoughts a mix of curiosity and uncertainty. The past few days had been filled with reflections on her expanded identity map, and she felt ready to share her progress with Elara, but she was also beginning to see new layers in her identity and lived experiences—layers she couldn't fully articulate yet.

Elara greeted her warmly, extending a hand toward the glowing mirror. With a graceful flick of her wrist, the light around the mirror seemed to pulse softly, illuminating a chair and inviting Mira to take her seat. "Welcome back, Mira. How have you been progressing with your reflections? Or perhaps I should ask—how has the *mirror of self* been treating you?"

Mira let out a small laugh as she settled into a chair. "Well, it's been... revealing, to say the least. I feel like I'm starting to see parts of myself more clearly, but at the same time, it's almost like the more I reflect, the more reflections I uncover. It's a bit overwhelming."

Elara chuckled softly. "That's the thing about mirrors—they show you more the longer you look. Our identities are much like an onion—each layer you peel back reveals something deeper underneath. Today, I want us to explore how different aspects of your identity become more or less important depending on the context you are in. We call this recognizing **salient identities**, or the key aspects of your identity that are most relevant in any particular context."

Mira frowned slightly, intrigued. "Salient identities?" she repeated.

Elara nodded. "Yes. At any given moment, depending on the context—whether it's where you are, who you're with, or what role you're playing—different aspects of your identity may become more prominent. This prominence is deeply tied to your positionality—how society has shaped your identity and the advantages or disadvantages it confers. For instance, your positionality as a White, well-educated woman brings both privilege and barriers that change depending on the environment you're in. Or, your gender might feel more salient when you're in a male-dominated environment, while your socioeconomic background might be more salient in situations involving financial decisions or conversations."

Elara extended her hand with a subtle point toward the mirror, and its surface rippled like water catching sunlight. Slowly, scenes from Mira's life began to emerge. Mira watched as her reflection changed—the young girl in a classroom where she was the only girl interested in engineering, the university student relying on scholarships to afford her education, and the professional engineer in a meeting dominated by men.

"Look at these moments," Elara said softly. "Can you see how different parts of your identity became more significant based on the context?"

Mira nodded slowly, her gaze fixed on the images. "In the engineering classes, my gender felt most significant. I always felt like I had to prove myself, as if my presence was under constant scrutiny. In college, my socioeconomic status became more prominent—I felt I needed to prove I deserved to be there because of my scholarship. The underrepresentation of women in engineering and financial inequities amplified both pressures. It wasn't just personal pressure but also the burden of systemic expectations."

Elara nodded. "Exactly. And these responses aren't always conscious. The systems we live in—**ideological, interpersonal,** and **institutional**—shape our behaviors in ways that seep into our subconscious. Even when we aren't actively thinking about these external pressures, our unconscious mind picks them up, and this can have powerful effects, creating the fourth *I* of the **Interlocking 4-I framework** you'll learn more about later in your journey, **internalized**."

Mira's eyes widened slightly. "Like **stereotype threat?**" she asked, her voice tentative.

Elara smiled. "Precisely. Stereotype threat is a perfect example. It's when you're aware of a stereotype about your group, and the fear of confirming that stereotype affects your performance or behavior. It's not always a conscious process—it's the unconscious mind reacting to those external pressures. These systems also affect our sense of **self-efficacy**—our belief in our ability to succeed. When stereotypes or biases are **internalized**, they can erode our confidence, making us attribute setbacks to personal failings rather than recognizing the systemic barriers at play. This can ultimately influence our **self-determination**, either by encouraging us to persist or by making us feel powerless."

Mira looked back at the image of herself in the classroom. She could see now how the fear of confirming stereotypes about women in engineering had held her back, even when she didn't fully realize it. "So, these systems get internalized," she said, "and they affect how I behave, even if I'm not fully aware of it."

"Exactly," Elara said. "And part of this journey is becoming aware of those internalized beliefs—recognizing when they're at play and challenging them. It's about understanding the conscious and unconscious forces shaping your actions. Context shapes which parts of our identity come to the forefront, and this awareness is crucial for understanding how we move through the world. Sometimes, our identities bring privilege; sometimes, they bring barriers. But there are also times when none of these identities are particularly salient, and we simply move through the moment without feeling the responsibility of those layers."

The mirror shimmered again, showing an image of Mira with her friends on a casual weekend hike. She was laughing, carefree, and focused on enjoying the time outdoors. "Here," Elara said, pointing at the image, "your identity as a woman, as a professional, as someone with a particular socioeconomic background—none of these were particularly significant in this context. You were simply Mira, enjoying time with your friends."

Mira smiled as she watched the scene. "It's true. I wasn't thinking about any of those things at that moment."

"Exactly," Elara said. "And that's the contrast. There are moments when your identity becomes salient, and there are moments when it fades into the background. Recognizing both allows you to understand when the context requires you to be mindful of those aspects and when you can simply be."

Elara paused, her hand sweeping through the air. The mirror glowed momentarily before revealing Mira in a meeting room, sitting silently. Mira watched the scene in the mirror. She saw herself hesitating to speak, her shoulders slightly hunched, her expression guarded.

"Think about this moment," Elara said gently. "Why did your gender feel so salient here in the meeting room?"

Mira frowned, her eyes narrowing as she considered the question. "I guess... it's because I've always felt like I had to work twice as hard to be taken seriously," she said slowly. "Especially in male-dominated spaces like this. It's like I've internalized the idea that my voice doesn't matter as much."

Elara nodded. "That's right. The external systems—like the cultural ideologies that prioritize male voices, the interpersonal dynamics in male-dominated environments, and the institutional practices that often overlook women's contributions—can become internalized. This internalization often manifests as **imposter syndrome**—a form of internalized oppression where individuals feel they are not deserving of their accomplishments, despite evidence of their competence. Imposter syndrome is not a personal flaw or a badge we should wear; it's a result of external systemic pressures that lead people, particularly those from **marginalized** groups (groups or individuals pushed to the edge of society through lack of access to rights, resources, and opportunities), to question and doubt their value. When we internalize these beliefs, they don't just influence our behaviors; they influence how we interact with others. Think of times you might have stayed quiet not because of your own doubt, but because of the way others perceived you. How did those interactions make you feel, and how did they shape your next steps?"

Mira's eyes widened slightly as she watched her reflection. "So, it's not just about what's happening at the moment—it's about all the messages I've absorbed over the years, often without even realizing it."

"Yes," Elara said. "Internalized beliefs are powerful because they shape how we see ourselves and how we move through the world. This doesn't only mean the internalization of limitations or inferiority; it also includes internalizing dominance or unwarranted superiority. Sometimes, people unconsciously adopt beliefs that their experiences, perspectives, or identities are more valid or important than others, and this, too, shapes interactions. Part of this journey is learning to recognize when those internalized beliefs—whether they are holding you back or giving you an unwarranted sense of superiority—are at play and challenging them."

The mirror shifted, showing Mira standing and speaking confidently in the same meeting. Elara smiled. "Every time you challenge those internalized beliefs, you create the possibility of a different outcome. The systems that shape us are real, but they're not immutable. You have the power to question them, to redefine them for yourself."

Mira nodded, conviction flickering in her eyes. She knew this was another piece of her journey—learning to identify the systems that influenced her, both externally and internally, consciously and unconsciously, and choosing how she would respond.

"Yes," Elara said with a smile. "When you understand which part of your identity is most salient, you can make more intentional choices—deciding when to lean into that identity, when to use it to create space for others, and when it might be influencing you in ways you need to be mindful of."

Mira looked at the mirror, her reflection shifting again. She saw herself in the manufacturing fabrication lab, standing back while a male colleague took the lead—a moment where she unconsciously deferred to him. Then the scene shifted—this time, Mira saw herself stepping forward, confidently taking the lead in the lab, demonstrating her technical skills, and guiding her team. By taking action, she was challenging internalized beliefs shaped by her positionality. Her actions were a way to resist systemic barriers that often placed women in the background, especially in STEM (Science, Technology, Engineering, and Math) environments.

"Every context offers you a choice," Elara said gently. "Recognizing what is salient helps you understand that choice and empowers you to act with intention."

Mira nodded, steadfastness shining in her eyes. She knew this was another piece of her journey—learning to be fully present, understanding how her identities played a role in every interaction, and using that awareness to navigate her world more consciously.

Pride lit up Elara's eyes as she smiled warmly. "Mira, that awareness is a powerful tool. Use it well. Next time, we will explore the systems of advantage and disadvantage that shape our lives and how they have influenced our journey."

Mira left the sanctuary that day with a renewed sense of purpose. She knew the work ahead would require her to continually reflect on her identity, to see beyond the surface, and to ask herself what was driving her actions. But she also knew she was capable of doing this work.

"One step at a time," she whispered to herself as she walked away from the sanctuary.

CHAPTER 8

Assess Salient Roles
MIRA'S REFLECTION

Over the next week, Mira thought constantly about her conversation with Elara. She had started noticing which parts of her identity felt most salient in different situations. It was like carrying a magnifying glass, illuminating parts of herself that she hadn't deeply explored before.

One afternoon at work, Mira hesitated to contribute during a technical meeting. She paused, her mind drifting back to her reflection with Elara. She realized that her gender felt most salient at that moment—an old habit of staying quiet because she doubted whether her voice would be valued in a male-dominated space.

As she observed the meeting, she watched Chanel speak up, though barely acknowledged. A few moments later, John repeated what Chanel had said, and the group suddenly acknowledged it. Mira felt a familiar frustration but knew she had a choice at that moment.

Mira decided to interject, her voice steady, "Actually, that's exactly what Chanel just said. We should ensure her perspective is fully understood before moving forward." The room went quiet for a moment before one of the senior engineers nodded, prompting Chanel to elaborate on her point. This time, Mira noticed a shift in the room—the attention seemed more focused, less dismissive. Mira felt a surge of energy; she realized that amplifying someone else's voice was a powerful step towards reshaping the group dynamic, but it was only part of the change needed to make the environment more inclusive.

That night, Mira wrote in her journal: *Today I realized my hesitation came from my gender feeling too salient in that space. But I chose to speak up anyway. Maybe that's what this is about—recognizing what holds me back and making the choice to step forward.*

Another day, Mira spoke with Quinn, a new colleague who openly discussed their journey as a **transgender** person in the workplace. Quinn shared how navigating the complexities of gender identity often meant evaluating how much of themselves they could safely share. Mira listened as Quinn talked about how their gender identity shaped interactions with colleagues—sometimes requiring them to manage people's assumptions about what it meant to be transgender.

Mira felt her own identity as a **cisgender** woman become salient. She realized she had never needed to explain or justify her gender; it had always been automatically accepted and unquestioned. Reflecting on Quinn's experience, Mira thought of her own cisgender privilege as a kind of *cloak of invisibility*—though far from shielding her from the societal scrutiny all women face, it allowed her gender to remain unquestioned and accepted without additional barriers or assumptions. For her, this invisibility was a source of ease, allowing her to navigate spaces without question. But she now understood that not everyone was afforded such a cloak.

For some transgender individuals, their gender identity might also allow them to move through the world invisibly, blending seamlessly into societal norms. But for others, especially those earlier in their transitions or those whose gender expressions don't align with societal expectations, their visibility could draw attention, scrutiny, or even harm. The absence of a cloak of invisibility can leave them vulnerable, navigating challenges Mira had never considered.

This realization deepened Mira's empathy. She recognized that her cloak of invisibility offered her a sense of ease but also limited her perspective, leaving her unaware of the barriers faced by others whose identities were constantly visible and often questioned. Instead of offering empty reassurances, Mira chose to listen, providing Quinn the space to share without judgment.

Later, Mira reflected: *Recognizing the salience of my identity helped me see Quinn's experience more clearly. The cloak of invisibility can be a source of ease, but its absence can mean constant visibility and scrutiny. By noticing when I have the privilege of invisibility, I can better connect with and support those for whom visibility—or lack of it—is a source of challenge. Sometimes, it's not about having the answers but about holding space for someone else's reality. Recognizing a salient identity allows me to connect more deeply, to understand where someone else might be coming from.*

By the end of the week, Mira could feel herself changing. She was still the same person, but she was becoming more aware of the people and environments around her—how some environments amplified her sense of belonging while others diminished it. She was more attuned to who she was in each moment, to which parts of her identity were at the forefront, and why. Mira began to realize that her changing awareness wasn't just about herself; it was about recognizing the structures that shaped her experiences, the privileges that eased her path, and the barriers that made certain spaces more challenging. The awareness wasn't always easy—it often came with discomfort, with the realization of how much she had held herself back. But it also came with power. The power to make different choices.

Mira closed her journal one evening, looking out the window at the darkening sky while petting Molly between her ears. She thought about what Elara had said—that recognizing what was salient offered her a choice. It wasn't about always making the perfect decision; it was about understanding herself well enough to act with intention. This awareness of her salient identities was a tool that helped her navigate spaces differently—understanding when she needed to speak up and when she could use her privilege to support others. Each choice was connected to an understanding of how her positionality gave her power in some contexts and limited her in others.

"One step at a time," she whispered, a smile touching her lips.

She knew she was ready for the next part of the journey. She had begun to understand herself, not just in isolation but in context. And now, she felt ready to learn about the systems of advantage and disadvantage that had shaped her life.

CHAPTER 9

Identify Bridges & Barriers
ELARA'S LESSON

Mira stepped into Elara's sanctuary once again, greeted by the familiar warmth and soft light. This time, she felt less hesitant and more assured. Her journal and parchment were tucked securely in her bag, with reflections from the past week still fresh in her mind. She had come to learn more, to continue her journey of understanding herself and her place in the world.

Elara smiled as Mira entered, resting her hand gently on the back of a nearby chair. A soft hum of energy flowed through the air, and the chair glided slightly forward, inviting Mira to sit. "Welcome back, Mira. You've been doing a lot of work. How are you feeling?"

Mira settled into her seat, taking a deep breath. "I've been... reflective," she said, a small smile tugging at her lips. "I've learned a lot about myself, but I also feel like there's more I don't yet understand."

Elara nodded kindly. "That's exactly why you're here today. We're going to dive deeper. You've explored different parts of who you are—now let's understand how these parts interact with

Identify Bridges and Barriers | LESSON

the world. You will consider the bridges that make your journey easier and the barriers that create obstacles."

As she extended her hand toward the mirror, the golden frame seemed to pulse softly with light, as if responding to her touch. The surface rippled like water touched by a gentle breeze, revealing scenes of workplaces, communities, and bustling cities. The images shifted seamlessly, each one alive with movement and detail. A faint hum filled the air, resonating from the mirror, as if the scenes carried their own energy. Elara's eyes flickered with warmth as she glanced at Mira, the light from the mirror casting a soft glow across her face.

"Today, we're going to explore **privilege** and **oppression**—**advantages** and **disadvantages**," Elara said. "These concepts help us understand how our identities fit into a larger social and political context. It's not just about who we are as individuals but about understanding where we stand within the systems that shape our opportunities and experiences. The real question we're asking today is: 'How do my identities shape the way I experience the world, and how does the world shape the opportunities or barriers I face?'"

Mira leaned in, her eyes following the images in the mirror. She saw a scene of herself and her college friends at a party, planning a spring break trip to Mexico. Everyone was excited except for Isabella. Considering her Mexican heritage, they thought she'd love the idea, but Mira noticed Isabella's hesitation. Isabella made excuses for not going, but it seemed unlike her. The real reason became clear years later—Isabella was a Dreamer, a child born in the U.S. to undocumented immigrants. Traveling outside the country wasn't possible or safe for her.

Elara turned to Mira, her expression subdued. "What you're seeing here is an experience faced by many people who carry different forms of disadvantage, often invisible to others. Isabella's hesitation—what did you notice about it?"

Mira watched the image replay, noticing Isabella's face shift from excitement to guardedness. "She seemed to shut down, like she had to distance herself," Mira said.

Elara nodded. "Exactly. Isabella's hesitation wasn't because she didn't want to go or didn't enjoy her friends' company. It was a practical decision rooted in her identity and circumstances—something others in the group didn't have to consider. Her disadvantage was invisible to those around her, yet it profoundly influenced her actions."

Mira watched the scene, her heart heavy as she realized how little she had understood at the time. Isabella's identity as an undocumented person shaped her choices in ways Mira hadn't recognized. It made her realize that privilege often means not having to think twice about decisions like travel while others face unseen barriers. The courage it must have taken for Isabella to navigate her daily life, knowing her limitations and risks, was immense.

"Privilege and oppression—these interconnected forces are often misunderstood," Elara continued, her tone steady and soothing. "Privilege doesn't mean you haven't worked hard. It means that there are aspects of your identity—like race, gender, socioeconomic background, nationality, or ability—that make your journey smoother by providing you with advantages others may not have. These bridges represent easier paths that many may take for granted. In contrast, oppression refers to the systemic barriers and disadvantages that prevent people from accessing the same opportunities. Understanding your positionality means recognizing how these advantages interact with the systems and structures in place. It's about seeing how the world often opens doors for some while closing them for others."

Mira swallowed, nodding slowly. "Like me being White," she said. "I suppose that's given me advantages, even if I haven't always noticed them."

Elara smiled gently. "Exactly. Privilege is often invisible to those who hold it because the systems in place are designed to make their experiences seem like the default. On the other hand, those who face systemic barriers are constantly reminded of them through everyday interactions—whether at work, school or even in social settings. Recognizing privilege requires stepping back and questioning what makes our path smoother while acknowledging that smoother doesn't mean it wasn't challenging or that you didn't struggle. It means certain barriers were absent for you that might exist for others. And understanding this is not about feeling guilt or shame—it's about awareness. It's about recognizing how we move through the world, what helps us and what hinders us, and understanding how these forces impact others differently."

The mirror shifted again, this time showing scenes from Mira's own life. She saw herself in high school, sitting in an advanced physics class with mostly boys. She saw her younger self, feeling out of place but pushing forward anyway. The image shifted to her at university, in a similar situation—trying to prove herself, trying to belong.

Mira watched, her chest tightening. "I've experienced some disadvantages, too," she said softly. "Being a woman in engineering, I know what it's like to be doubted, to feel like you have to prove yourself over and over."

"Yes," Elara said, her voice full of empathy. "You've faced disadvantages because of your gender, just as others face disadvantages for their race, socioeconomic background, ability status, religion, or other dimensions of identity. These elements can create either bridges or barriers in our lives. The systems we navigate every day are often designed to privilege some while creating obstacles for others."

Mira turned away from the mirror, meeting Elara's eyes. "How do I learn to see these systems more clearly?" she asked.

Elara smiled. "It starts with awareness. You've already begun—understanding your identity and how it fits into the broader world. Learning to see systems will become easier as you continue through the **Positionality Practices**. For now, the next step is to question—who benefits in each situation? Who gets a bridge, and who faces barriers? Reflect on the privileges you hold, the disadvantages you've faced, and how they shape your interactions."

Mira nodded, her mind swirling with thoughts. "It's like... everything is connected. My identity, the privileges I have, the disadvantages I face—they all affect how I see the world and how others see me."

"Precisely," Elara said. "This understanding will help you navigate the world with more empathy, with more insight. It will help you see beyond your own experiences, to recognize the unseen forces at play, and to use that awareness to be a better ally, a better leader, and a better person."

Elara gestured toward the glowing mirror, her expression becoming more serious. "Mira, what I'm about to show you will help you understand how bridges and barriers manifest in our lives. It will give you a clearer picture of how different factors can either support us or weigh us down." The mirror shimmered again, revealing a new scene. Mira leaned in, her curiosity piqued.

The scene showed an image of herself wearing a large backpack[3] on her shoulders. It appeared almost weightless, filled with various objects poking out of the top—maps, keys, and tools that shimmered with a warm glow. Behind her, Mira also saw a series of bridges and barriers. Some bridges were well-built, solid, and easy to access and cross, while others were crumbling or incomplete. In contrast, barriers appeared as large walls or broken paths, blocking the way. Elara spoke as Mira watched.

"Think of privilege like this backpack, Mira," Elara said. "It's filled with resources you can use in your life—things you may

Identify Bridges and Barriers | LESSON 59

not have even noticed were there because they have always been available to you. These resources represent unearned advantages—tools that help you navigate the world more easily. Similarly, think of the bridges you see. Some of us have well-built bridges that make our journeys smoother—connections that help us cross obstacles without even realizing they exist. On the other hand, barriers can block the paths for others, making progress more difficult or even impossible without support."

The mirror zoomed in on the backpack, and one by one, the objects inside became clear. A map with directions to an office building, labeled with words like 'Housing Choice,' 'Educational Access,' and 'Representation.' Each word glowed softly. The image then shifted to the bridges—some labeled 'Mentorship,' 'Community Support,' and 'Financial Stability.' These bridges represented the pathways that allowed Mira to move forward more easily, showing how advantages connect to opportunities.

"These are examples of advantages you might carry without even being aware," Elara continued. "The ability to find housing in neighborhoods that feel safe, and that you can afford. Access to expansive educational opportunities. The ability to see yourself widely represented in media. The assurance that when you speak, others are more likely to listen because of who you are. Each of these makes your journey smoother in ways that aren't always obvious."

Mira's expression shifted as the image changed again, now with an image of Isabella, her shoulders burdened with a heavy backpack filled with weights labeled 'Travel Restrictions,' 'Fear of Exposure,' and 'Lack of Representation.' Alongside Isabella were broken or incomplete bridges labeled 'Lack of Documentation' and 'Limited Resources' and barriers like 'Legal Obstacles.' Mira's heart sank as she realized that while she carried tools and crossed bridges to move forward, others like Isabella carried weights and faced barriers that slowed them down or made certain paths impossible to travel.

Elara continued, "The point is not to feel guilty for what you have, Mira. The point is to be aware that not everyone carries the same tools, and some carry burdens you might never see. Not everyone has the same path. By recognizing the difference, you can begin to use your own advantages to help remove those burdens, or at least make space for others to navigate their own journey."

Mira nodded slowly, absorbing the imagery. She could now see that understanding these differences wasn't just an intellectual exercise but a call to action. She had privileges she hadn't recognized before, and now, with awareness, she had a choice to use them with intention.

Elara pointed once again to Mira's journal. "Today, I want you to begin a new exercise. Reflect on the bridges and barriers, the advantages and disadvantages, that have shaped your journey. Consider dimensions of your identity such as race, gender, socioeconomic status, religion, ability, language, and more. Reflect on how these aspects have influenced your opportunities or presented obstacles. There is no right or wrong here, only reflection. Use the table to help you."

Mira took the parchment, her eyes meeting Elara's once more. "I think this is making more sense. It's not just about who I am—it's about who I am within this world, with all its history and complexity. It's the roads I've walked, the bridges and barriers I've experienced, and what I carry, both visible and invisible."

Elara nodded. "Exactly. Once you understand that, you'll start to see how you can make a difference—not just for yourself, but for others as well. This understanding of what we carry and what others might not have access to helps us empathize, and it can guide our actions toward creating **equity**."

Mira felt a new resolve welling up within her. This journey challenged her, pushing her to confront uncomfortable truths, but it also opened her eyes in ways she had never imagined. She was ready to keep going.

"Thank you, Elara," she said, her voice steady.

Elara smiled. "One step at a time, Mira. You're doing the work, and that's what matters."

"One step at a time," she repeated, her mind already turning to the reflection she would do tonight.

Exploring Dimensions of Identity: Bridges, Barriers, and Systems of Oppression

The table on the following page spread highlights 12 key identity dimensions, showing how privilege (bridges) and oppression (barriers) shape access, opportunity, and experiences. It also identifies the systems of oppression that sustain these dynamics. While not exhaustive of identities or examples of advantages/disadvantages, the table serves as a starting point for reflection and action, with the understanding that identities and systems evolve over time.

MAGIC MIRROR

Dimension of Identity	Group(s) WITH Advantage	Group(s) WITHOUT Advantage	Advantages of Privilege (Bridges)	Disadvantages of Oppression (Barriers)	System of Oppression (-isms)
Race	White	Black, Indigenous, People of Color	Easier access to housing, jobs, and legal fairness	Disproportionate policing, racial discrimination	Racism
Ethnicity / Ancestral Heritage	Western European Heritage	Historically Devalued Lineages	Cultural norms and narratives align with the dominant group	Stereotyping, cultural erasure	Ethnocentrism
Religion / Spirituality	Christian, Catholic	Non-Christian Faiths (e.g., Jewish, Muslim, Hindu), Atheists, Agnostics	Defaulted holidays and schedules, social acceptance	Faith-based exclusion, religious prejudice	Religious Discrimination (Anti-Semitism, Islamophobia)
Biological Sex	Male	Female, Intersex, Transsexual	Assumed competence, higher earning potential	Gender pay gap, fewer leadership opportunities	Sexism
Gender Identity	Cisgender	Transgender, Non-Conforming	Legal documentation matches identity, social recognition	Deadnaming, discrimination in healthcare	Transphobia
Gender Expression	Masculine	Feminine, Androgynous, Non-Conforming	Fit into societal gender norms, fewer challenges	Stereotyping, lack of flexibility in dress codes	Gender Binarism

Identify Bridges and Barriers | LESSON 63

Dimension of Identity	Group(s) WITH Advantage	Group(s) WITHOUT Advantage	Advantages of Privilege (Bridges)	Disadvantages of Oppression (Barriers)	System of Oppression (-isms)
Sexual Orientation	Heterosexual	LGBTQ+ Identities	Relationship status legally recognized, assumed normalcy	Stigma, lack of legal protections	Heterosexism (Homophobia, Biphobia)
Class / Economic Status	Upper/ Middle Class	Working Class, Individuals in Poverty	Wealth leads to better education, healthcare access	Limited upward mobility, job precarity	Classism
Educational Level	Graduate Degree Holders	First-Generation College Students, GED Holders	Assumed expertise, greater career opportunities	Fewer professional networks, credential barriers	Educational Elitism
Physical Ability	Able-Bodied	Individuals with Disabilities	Full access to spaces, low-cost health needs	Physical barriers, inaccessible environments	Ableism
Psychological Ability	Mentally and Emotionally Adept	Individuals with Mental Health Challenges	No stigma in professional or social settings	Limited accommodations, workplace discrimination	Ableism (Sanism, Mentalism)
Appearance	Physically Attractive, Thin (Aligned with Social Norms)	Individuals Perceived as "Unattractive" or Divergent from Beauty Norms	Favorable treatment in hiring, social acceptance	Bias in hiring, ridicule or judgment based on looks	Appearance-Based Discrimination (Lookism)

CHAPTER 10

Identify Bridges & Barriers
MIRA'S REFLECTION

The next week unfolded in a quiet yet profound series of realizations. Mira spent her days moving through her regular routines—work, errands, time with friends—but something had shifted within her. She carried with her a different awareness, a new lens through which she saw her surroundings, her interactions, and herself.

Each morning, she opened her journal, revisiting her social identity map and reflecting on her advantages and disadvantages. It felt like an evolving conversation, prompting her to reconsider her life—from the opportunities she had taken for granted to the barriers she had overcome.

One day at work, Mira noticed the dynamics during a team meeting. It was subtle, almost invisible, but she could see it clearly now—the way her male colleagues spoke freely, without hesitation, while some of the women, herself included, chose their words carefully or stayed quiet altogether. It was an unspoken imbalance, a reminder of how gender shaped the space people occupied. Mira reflected on this later, noting in her journal: *The confidence gap isn't just personal—it's systemic. How can I use my position to help make this space more equitable for everyone?*

She remembered her conversations with Elara about privilege and disadvantage and began to notice the advantages she often overlooked: her car, her ability to avoid public transportation, and even her name, which fit cultural norms and was typically easy enough to pronounce, though people still called her *my-rah* instead of *mee-rah* at times. She realized how much that simple fact had likely helped her during interviews and first impressions. It made her think about how different her experience would have been if she had a name that stood out or was considered 'difficult' to pronounce. Each of these aspects was a reminder of how her positionality influenced not just her opportunities but also how others perceived her. These privileges were so ingrained in her daily life that she had never recognized them as privileges before. Now, they were like little flags waving, reminding her of the things she didn't have to struggle for.

Later in the week, Mira met her friend Ruby at a coffee shop. This time, she listened differently, seeing the layers of frustration and systemic disadvantages her friend faced because of her race and gender. Mira began to understand the exhausting barriers that she hadn't fully grasped before.

In the middle of the conversation, however, Mira slipped. Her friend described how she was overlooked for a promotion, and Mira quickly interjected, "Maybe if you worked a bit harder or spoke up more, they would notice you." Her friend paused, giving her a patient smile, but Mira could sense the exhaustion behind it.

Later that night, sitting with her journal, Mira realized her mistake. Though she meant to be helpful, she had reduced her friend's struggle to a matter of personal effort, ignoring the systemic barriers at play. Mira wrote in her journal: *I need to remember that it's not always about working harder. Systems of advantage and disadvantage shape outcomes in ways that aren't always visible, especially to those who benefit from the system. I need to recognize these structures and validate the experiences of those facing barriers rather than offering simplistic solutions.*

Later that week, Mira met with another colleague, James, who often spoke about the challenges of balancing work with caring for his elderly parents. Mira wanted to offer support but found herself hesitating. When she finally asked how she could help, James seemed distant, his expression guarded.

"Thanks, Mira," he said, a hint of tension in his voice. "But I think sometimes people just want to be understood, not fixed."

Mira felt her cheeks flush. She realized that her positionality—having a support system and financial stability—made it difficult to fully understand James's strain. She had assumed she could offer solutions, but James needed empathy. This conversation stayed with her, and that evening, she wrote in her journal: *I need to remember that my experience isn't universal. Sometimes, the best way to support someone is to be there without trying to solve things for them. I must recognize when my privileges limit my ability to connect with others.*

As the week continued, she also thought about the children from the neighborhood—those who had asked if they could fish in her backyard. She thought about how easily she had said no, not just because of the liability concern but also because of what her neighbors might think. Mira realized that her position of ownership, the privilege of having access to the lake, gave her the power to decide who could enjoy it and who couldn't. She wondered what it would mean to share that advantage more equitably. She wrote in her journal: *Sometimes privilege isn't just about what you have—it's about what you decide to do with it.*

Mira also had more difficult moments of personal reflection. One evening, while preparing dinner, she thought about her ethnicity—how she had distanced herself from her Hispanic roots to fit in, choosing acceptance over authenticity. She thought about how that choice had given her certain advantages, like avoiding stereotypes or feeling more accepted by her predominantly White peers. But it had also meant a loss, a distancing from her heritage and culture. This journey of understanding her personhood was, she realized, an ongoing process, one without a finish line. She knew there would always be new realizations, new pieces of herself to uncover.

Toward the end of the week, Mira returned to her journal and noticed a pattern. She recognized how her privileges afforded her unexamined opportunities while her disadvantages had forced her to adapt. The most significant realization was that this process was not about reaching an endpoint—it was about continuous growth, an ongoing cycle of reflection, awareness, and adjustment.

Mira was beginning to see herself differently, which also made her more aware of the people around her. She wondered if this awareness marked the beginning of what Elara described as the next part of her journey: Perception. To truly make a difference, she needed to understand how others saw the world and how they saw her. Her experiences were just one piece of the puzzle; understanding others would require stepping beyond her own perspective and positionality.

For now, she knew that understanding her Personhood would remain an essential part of her journey—an ongoing practice of recognizing, questioning, and understanding the forces that shaped her life. She felt ready for the next step: to move beyond her viewpoint and truly understand the experiences of those around her. It was a question she was eager to explore, even if the answers would take time.

She sat with these questions, feeling both overwhelmed and motivated. These weeks had shown her that there was so much more to learn, so much more to understand. And that, she realized, was the point. There was no end to this journey. The reflection on Personhood would continue, just as she would begin to learn about her Perception—the way she moved through the world, the way she saw others, and the way they saw her.

Mira closed her journal and looked out the window, the evening sky was streaked with the colors of a fiery pink sunset. She felt a sense of anticipation, knowing she was on the brink of another chapter in her journey.

"One step at a time," she whispered, a small smile touching her lips as the sky darkened outside. "I'm ready."

POSITIONALITY PRISM PART 2
Perception

CHAPTER 11

Check Your Filter

ELARA'S LESSON

A few weeks later, when Mira returned to Elara's sanctuary, her mind was buzzing with curiosity about what would come next. The last part of her journey had been transformative, allowing her to map out her personhood and understand the interplay of her identities. But today, she sensed a shift—a different kind of journey lay ahead.

Elara greeted her warmly, standing beside the glowing mirror, which now seemed to pulse with an energy that was almost alive. The air felt charged, as if something extraordinary was about to happen.

"Welcome back, Mira," Elara said, her eyes twinkling. "Are you ready for the next step?"

Mira nodded, her gaze shifting to the mirror. "Yes, I think so. What are we doing today?"

Elara smiled. "Today, we move into **Perception**—how you see others and how they see you. This is the second piece of the Positionality Prism. To do this, we need to explore bias and prejudice. **Bias** isn't inherently bad; it's part of how our brains are wired to make sense of the world quickly. Think of bias like a mental shortcut—our brains use past experiences and learned patterns to form judgments in an instant. For example, you might instinctively assume a barking dog is dangerous because of stories you've heard or past experiences. **Prejudice**, on the other hand, is a preconceived opinion not based on reason or actual experience. For instance, deciding you dislike a culture's cuisine without ever trying it is prejudice, not bias. But these shortcuts can also mislead us, especially when they're shaped by stereotypes, incomplete, or false information."

"Oh!" Mira interrupted. "When I found my sweet Molly dog dumped to fend for herself on my road, I admit I was scared of her. She was a beautiful little blue nose pitbull puppy, but I'd never spent time with pits, especially pitbull puppies, and I'd heard terrible things! She is super playful, though, and, initially, very rough and bitey. I really thought she might hurt me! Then, I got to know her and taught her how to interact with humans. I was biased by negative stereotypes about her breed, and I feel sad to think that I almost let stereotypes lead me to give up a great dog." Mira chuckles and then adds, "I've had Molly for a year, but my mom still jokes that all of Molly's incessant licks are just an attempt to tenderize her to eat someday. In reality, Molly is the snuggliest, happiest, and biggest lapdog ever."

Elara nodded thoughtfully. "Mira, that's a powerful example. Molly's story shows how biases, even subtle ones, can influence our reactions. The good news is that the brain also supports the self-regulation of cognitive control, which can reduce the expression of prejudice and stereotypes. And just like you unlearned the stereotypes about Molly's breed, we can work to recognize and challenge our biases about people." She paused, her tone growing firmer. "When biases extend to people and are shaped by stereotypes or harmful ideologies, they can lead to unfair judgments and reinforce societal divides. This is when bias becomes problematic, especially when it creates an 'us vs. them' mentality, and leads to **discrimination**, the unjust or prejudicial treatment of different categories of people."

"Our positionality acts like a filter," Elara continued. "We interpret everything through our identity and lived experiences. This filter shapes our biases, affects our reactions, and guides how we engage with the world. Unless we intentionally change it, the filter will influence us automatically. Today, you'll understand how these biases operate—intellectually and viscerally because the mirror will act as a portal this time."

Mira took a deep breath, her gaze flickering between Elara and the mirror. The idea of the mirror as a portal both thrilled and unsettled her. "A portal?" she asked, her voice tinged with a mix of wonder and trepidation. "What will it show me?" For a moment, doubt crept in. Could she handle what lay ahead? Shaking off the hesitation, she nodded, determination softening her apprehension. "I guess I'm ready," she whispered, though her pulse quickened in anticipation.

Elara stepped back, her voice a whisper of the wind. "Close your eyes, Mira. Trust the mirror. It will guide you."

Mira closed her eyes, feeling the warmth of the mirror wash over her, like sunlight seeping through her skin. The surface beneath her feet seemed to dissolve, replaced by a weightless sensation, as if she were suspended in midair. Colors and light swirled around her, dancing like shimmering ribbons in a vast, endless expanse. The faint hum of energy filled her ears, vibrating softly in her chest. Then, she felt a firm but subtle pull, like a placid current carrying her forward. It wasn't frightening, but it was deeply unfamiliar—a sensation of being simultaneously grounded and untethered. Her heart raced as she surrendered to the motion, allowing herself to float into the unknown. When she opened her eyes, she was no longer in the sanctuary.

Instead, she stood in a bustling office—except she wasn't herself. She could feel her body was different, her perspective shifting as she stood in a different context, feeling how her surroundings affected her. She looked down and realized she was inhabiting the body of Lisa, a young Black colleague she knew well. Dressed in business attire, she stood in front of a large conference room with her colleagues. Her heart raced, and she could sense the intensity of the stares from around the room.

Mira could feel the difference in how Lisa was perceived compared to how she was usually treated in similar settings as a White woman. There was a skepticism in the air, a hesitation she had rarely encountered herself. Someone in the meeting, a middle-aged White man, spoke over her as she began to present. Mira could feel the sting of the interruption, the subtle dismissiveness in his tone, the way his voice seemed to carry an authority that automatically drew attention, replacing her words with his own. Despite her attempts to re-engage, her contributions were minimized, as if she were invisible.

The frustration was palpable, pressing against Mira as she embodied Lisa. Mira felt Lisa's urge to speak up and demand attention, but hesitation restrained her—a hesitation rooted in Lisa's lived experiences. Mira could feel Lisa's internal dialogue as if it were her own: the fear of being labeled with the harmful 'angry Black woman' stereotype. This wasn't an abstract fear—it was a reality Lisa had faced before. Mira, through Lisa's perspective, recalled the discomfort in her colleagues' eyes when her passion was misunderstood as aggression, how even her assertiveness could be reframed as hostility. Lisa had learned to temper her voice, to avoid raising it even slightly, knowing how easily it could feed into the biases others carried about her.

Mira noticed another interaction—a young White woman touched Lisa's hair without asking, commenting on how 'wildly cool' it looked. Despite being framed as a compliment, the casual invasion of Lisa's personal space felt condescending and disrespectful. There was an implication behind the word 'wild' that suggested Lisa's natural hair was somehow unprofessional or untamed, playing into long-standing stereotypes about Black hair. These stereotypes carry a deep history, rooted in the idea that certain types of hair are 'acceptable' or 'professional' while others are not—a reality that continues to affect many Black individuals today. Mira could feel Lisa's discomfort, the calculation of whether to address it or let it go to avoid making others uncomfortable. These subtle **microaggressions** wore Lisa down, making her workplace exhausting.

As she stood there, her mind flashed with the term **confirmation bias**. She realized the people in the room likely had preconceived notions about Lisa's abilities—ideas that were not based on her skills or contributions but rather on stereotypes they carried about Black women in professional spaces. Mira also saw a colleague giving Lisa unsolicited advice in a condescending tone, assuming she needed help with her presentation. These subtle jabs chipped away at Lisa's confidence, emphasizing the constant pressure to prove her worth in a space that doubted her from the outset.

The scene began to shift subtly. The bustling office blurred, colors melding into streaks of light. A moment later, she found herself back in Elara's sanctuary, the warm glow of the mirror steadying her. Mira's body tensed as if she carried Lisa's exhaustion with her. She turned toward Elara, who now stood beside her, a serene presence amidst the storm of emotions swirling inside.

Mira began to see how her own positionality—her identity as a White woman with the privilege of navigating predominantly White spaces—had influenced her understanding of such moments. She had always believed confidence was enough to succeed in the workplace because the friction she faced was different for her. However, for Lisa, confidence wasn't the issue. It was the systemic barriers, the deeply rooted assumptions others held about her abilities before she even opened her mouth—assumptions shaped by overlapping racial and gender biases that Mira rarely faced.

Mira's mind drifted to her friend Ruby and the subtle moments of tension in their conversations. Ruby had once shared a vulnerable story about a workplace incident, her voice tinged with frustration. At the time, Mira had felt unsure of how to respond and thus didn't. Looking back now, she realized she had dismissed Ruby's lived experience without fully listening or understanding. She had fallen into the same patterns of minimizing or redirecting discomfort.

The weight of the realization settled heavily on Mira's shoulders. She stood in the sanctuary, the glow of the mirror reflecting her inner turmoil. For a moment, she remained silent, gathering her thoughts and piecing together the connections between what she had experienced and what she now understood. Finally, she turned to Elara, her voice tinged with both vulnerability and resolve. "It's not just Lisa or my friend, Ruby," she thought. "It's my own reluctance to confront these systems and my complicity in them. I've let these moments pass without action, without even acknowledging the harm."

Mira thought back to her own experiences again and realized, with discomfort, that she had made assumptions about Black women being 'angry' or 'difficult.' These fleeting thoughts, buried deep, were remnants of stereotypes she had absorbed unknowingly. A wave of guilt washed over her as she acknowledged them, and with her head drooped down in despair, a tear escaped from the corner of her eye and fell on her wringing hands.

Mira remembered a particular interaction with her colleague, Danielle, who was also Black. They had worked together on a project, and Mira had been surprised by Danielle's directness in meetings. At the time, she interpreted it as Danielle being 'too aggressive'—a fleeting thought influenced by internalized stereotypes. The realization made her uncomfortable. Had she allowed that bias to affect their collaboration? Had she failed to give Danielle's ideas the weight they deserved because of her assumptions?

Mira reflected aloud, her voice filled with concern. "I must be more intentional about catching these biases before they influence my actions. Danielle's assertiveness is her strength, but my positionality has made me see it through a biased lens. I need to unpack these thoughts and ensure they don't stand in the way of truly collaborating and connecting with my colleagues."

Elara spoke gently in response, magically having heard Mira's internal reflective dialogue about Lisa, Ruby, and Danielle. "These biases are not just your own, Mira. They are part of the underlying and insidious ideologies that our society perpetuates—ideas about who deserves to be heard, who gets to be assertive, and who is seen as a threat. These biases are woven into our institutions, our media, and our education system—they shape the narratives we hear from a young age about race, gender, and power. Even if we openly reject these narratives, they still find a way to influence our subconscious. Recognizing them and where they come from is crucial, not just to change yourself, but to begin challenging these systems more broadly."

Mira nodded slowly, her vulnerability outweighing her determination. "I think I... I'm starting to see it. Confidence alone isn't enough—but I still don't fully understand. These systems, these ideologies... they feel so big, so overwhelming. I don't know how to start unraveling them or where I fit into all of it."

Elara stepped forward and gently touched Mira's shoulder, her gaze warm and encouraging. "You're doing well, Mira," she said softly. "Each step you take brings more clarity. The mirror will guide you again, and this next journey will offer a new perspective—one that builds on everything you've started to uncover. Trust yourself and trust the mirror. You've already shown courage, even in your uncertainty."

Mira took a deep breath and stepped closer to the glowing surface. The air around her shimmered, and she felt a familiar pull, the sensation of being drawn through light and space.

The scene changed again, and Mira found herself in a brightly lit classroom, inhabiting the body of Mr. Harrison, an early childhood educator. She saw colorful storybooks, small chairs, and children's art decorating the walls. Mira felt Mr. Harrison's deep sense of pride and purpose—the joy of nurturing young minds.

But Mira also sensed Mr. Harrison's barriers—whispers among parents, subtle doubts about why a man would work with young children. These assumptions carried notions about masculinity and questioned his intentions. Mira felt the exhaustion of constantly needing to prove himself simply because he didn't fit the expected mold of an early childhood educator.

As she stepped into Mr. Harrison's shoes, Mira realized how powerful the stereotypes were—how they cast a shadow over every interaction, making even simple acts of kindness or care subject to suspicion. The implicit bias wasn't just from the parents; it came from colleagues too—people who subtly belittled his work as not being "real teaching" or as less significant compared to their roles. The frustration built up inside her, and Mira felt Mr. Harrison's struggle to maintain his passion with the doubts surrounding him.

Mira felt the gravity of these biases, recognizing the **fundamental attribution error** at play—the tendency for others to attribute Mr. Harrison's career choice to something unusual or wrong about his character rather than acknowledging his genuine passion and dedication to teaching young children. The biases held against him weren't about his qualifications or abilities; they were rooted in societal expectations about gender roles, expectations that Mr. Harrison had to fight every day.

The mirror flashed, and Mira felt herself being pulled back through the swirling currents of light and color. Her body became heavier as the weightlessness dissolved, and with a final rush of warmth, she was back in her body, standing in front of Elara. Her breath was shaky, and a wave of emotion—frustration, sadness, anger—washed over her like a tidal surge, leaving her momentarily unsteady. "That was... intense," she managed, her voice cracking.

Elara nodded, her eyes filled with empathy. "Bias is powerful, Mira. It's not just something we think—it's something we feel. It shapes how we move through the world and how others respond to us."

Mira swallowed, her hands trembling slightly. "It felt so powerless. No matter what they did, it felt like Mr. Harrison and Lisa couldn't change the perceptions other people had of them."

Elara nodded. "That is the reality for so many people. Bias is not just an individual feeling—it's connected to broader societal ideologies. These ideologies are ingrained in our culture, institutions, and personal experiences. They shape what we expect from others and what they expect from us."

Mira nodded, her mind spinning. "So, it's not just about my biases—it's about the systems that create them, the ideologies that keep them alive. And my own lived experience—it's like I've been shielded from seeing some of these systems. Shielded from seeing my own brain's biases."

Elara's gaze softened, and she gestured toward the mirror. "Let's return to another moment, one that might offer further clarity. Do you remember your conversation with Ruby at the café? The emotions you felt then are deeply tied to what we're exploring now."

Mira's heart sank slightly as the memory surfaced. "I do. Ruby was sharing her struggles at work, and... I cried. It wasn't even about her story directly—it was about how it made me feel about myself. I realized I might not be the friend I thought I was, and

I felt overwhelmed. But I didn't say anything meaningful to her. I just... let the moment slip away."

Elara nodded thoughtfully. "Your tears carried a weight, Mira. They weren't just tears of empathy—they were tied to your discomfort, specifically your discomfort talking about race and your confrontation with a fear of inadequacy. Ruby's experience highlighted something you weren't ready to face: how your silence can unintentionally center yourself instead of offering her the space and support she needed."

Mira winced at the memory, her voice quiet. "I think Ruby noticed. She changed the subject, and I didn't know how to fix it."

Elara's tone remained gentle but firm. "This is where the concept of **white fragility** and what some call '**white women's tears**' comes into play. It's not that your emotions were wrong or invalid, but when they become the focus, they can shift the emotional labor onto the person sharing their experience. Ruby's annoyance wasn't about your tears as much as it was about the dynamic they created—the way they redirected the moment."

Mira looked at the mirror, her reflection steady yet unfamiliar. "I've read about these ideas before, but living them... It's different. It's uncomfortable."

"And that discomfort," Elara said, stepping closer, "is where growth begins. It's tied to the 'us versus them' ideologies we spoke of earlier—the invisible lines that define who is deserving of comfort, who carries the burden of making others feel okay. Your café interaction mirrored a broader dynamic that you've seen in other moments, too."

Mira's voice steadied, determination creeping into her tone. "I see it now. I let my emotions and silence become part of the problem. I need to do better—not just feel better. Next time, I can pause, take a breath, and make sure my response centers on the other person instead of my own feelings."

Check Your Filter | LESSON   81

Elara smiled gently. "That's a step forward. Awareness leads to intentional action. And intentional action leads to change—not just within yourself but in the systems you navigate and influence."

Her voice trailed off as a memory from the outreach event surfaced unbidden. She glanced at Elara, her face a mixture of guilt and curiosity. "There was this moment," she began, "at a STEM outreach event I volunteered at. A fellow volunteer said something that didn't sit right with me—about 'these kids' needing 'us' to bring nature to them. It felt... wrong, but I didn't say anything. I just smiled and let it go."

Elara tilted her head slightly, her expression encouraging. "What does it feel like to revisit that moment?"

Mira hesitated, then sighed. "It's clear now what bothered me. The way she spoke created an 'us versus them' dynamic. It wasn't just the words—it was the subtext, the unspoken assumption that these kids lacked something and we were their saviors. But instead of challenging it, I stayed silent. I didn't want to make waves."

Elara nodded thoughtfully. "And how does that moment connect to what you've experienced and learned today?"

Mira's eyes widened slightly. "It's the same pattern, isn't it? That instinct to protect comfort—mine or someone else's—over speaking up against harmful biases. I've been so afraid of being seen as overreacting or confrontational that I've let these moments pass. But now, after seeing Lisa's and Mr. Harrison's experiences, I understand the cost of silence. It reinforces the very systems I want to challenge."

"Exactly," Elara said gently. "Awareness is powerful, Mira, but action transforms. What could you do differently next time?"

Mira straightened, determination in her voice. "I need to name what I see, even if it's uncomfortable. I can ask questions to challenge those subtexts, like 'What makes you say that?' or

'How can we think about this differently?' It's not just about **calling out**—it's about **calling in**."

Elara smiled. "That's a start. Reflection gives you clarity, and clarity fuels courage. Let's carry this awareness forward as we prepare for the next step."

Elara nodded thoughtfully as she shifted the conversation. "It's hard to see the systems when, in many ways, they were built for you. When you don't experience the friction, it's easy to assume others are overreacting or simply not trying hard enough. This connects directly to your café interaction with Ruby and the STEM outreach event. Both illustrate how systemic dynamics and biases shape our responses and reinforce divides. But the reality is different. For those facing systemic barriers, the constant need to prove oneself is not about weakness—it's about enduring the weight of biased expectations and still showing up every day. Recognizing that shield is a powerful first step, Mira. Our positionality is like a filter—it influences everything we see and do. Recognizing your biases is the first step of **Perception**, but you must also understand where they come from—the cultural norms, stereotypes, and histories that shape them. It's also important to recognize how your positionality—your identity as a White woman, your experiences in a male-dominated field—shapes your perspective, your areas of unawareness, and your reactions. Only then can you begin to unravel these biases, to challenge them."

Mira paused, reflecting deeply. "I might hold biases against Black women or make assumptions about men in early childcare—all based on my lived experiences in a society that favors the dominant culture. Even if I reject these biases openly, they can still exist subconsciously and affect my behavior. Awareness is the first step, but intentional action is next, right?"

"That's right, Mira. That's right. But before we end today, I want to encourage you to continue this journey of awareness.

Journal over the next week noting any instances where you make quick judgments about others—reflecting on what might be behind those thoughts and how your positionality may act as a filter in shaping those judgments. Connect these biases to the larger systems or ideologies we discussed today. While doing so, be careful not to center yourself and your emotions, as you did unconsciously with Ruby in the café. Instead, focus on creating space for understanding."

Elara continued, "When we meet again, we'll begin the next practice of our journey: **empathy-driven perspective-taking**. Recognizing bias is one thing, but using empathy to shift perspectives intentionally is another. I think you'll find this an empowering and enlightening next step."

CHAPTER 12

Check Your Filter
MIRA'S REFLECTION

Mira sat at her kitchen table, her journal open before her, her pen resting lightly on the page, and Molly resting at her feet. She had written a prompt at the top of the page: *Reflections on Filters and Judgments*. She took a deep breath, closed her eyes, and let her mind wander back to the experiences she had lived through the mirror.

She thought about Lisa in the conference room—the way her voice had been drowned out, the way her contributions had been dismissed. The feeling of invisibility lingered, the frustration of not being heard. Mira picked up her pen and wrote:

Today, I experienced what it feels like to be minimized because of someone else's bias. It wasn't about the validity of my words, but about how I was perceived—a reflection of deeper cultural beliefs that often silence Black women in professional spaces. This wasn't just one person's bias; it was part of a broader societal ideology that undervalues voices like mine.

The confirmation bias of those around me prevented them from recognizing Lisa's valuable contributions. It struck me that her strug-

gles weren't about her competence but about deeply ingrained perceptions shaped by the system we live in. Society subtly teaches whose voices deserve authority and whose don't, reinforcing barriers that have nothing to do with merit and everything to do with bias.

I also thought about Mr. Harrison in the classroom and the stereotypes he faced simply because of his choice to work in early childhood education. As I reflected, I realized how my own positionality influences my perceptions. Being a woman in a male-dominated field meant I understood the struggle to overcome stereotypes, but I hadn't considered how my assumptions about traditional gender roles might lead me to see Mr. Harrison's work differently. The biases held against him weren't about his abilities but were rooted in societal expectations about gender roles—expectations that I, too, had internalized without questioning. The fundamental attribution error led others to make assumptions about his character rather than recognizing his passion and dedication. These experiences have made me realize how these biases are deeply embedded in our society and how they impact people differently based on their identity.

Mira set her pen down, her eyes misty. She realized that bias wasn't just something that happened in the abstract—it was something that shaped lives, that caused pain and frustration. It was something that she needed to confront, not just in others, but within herself.

She picked up her pen again, writing at the bottom of the page:

What biases do I carry? How have they influenced the way I see others? How does my positionality act as a filter that shapes my perceptions? What ideologies have shaped these biases, and how can I begin to challenge them?

Mira closed her journal, her heart heavy with the enormity of the questions. She knew this was just the beginning. The mirror had shown her the world through someone else's eyes, and now it was time to turn that lens inward, to examine her own biases and her own beliefs, and to begin the work of changing them.

She realized that recognizing her positionality was not a one-time reflection, but an ongoing practice—one that would require her to stay vigilant, compassionate, and committed. She knew that moving beyond awareness required intentional action: using her power, privilege, and position to challenge these biases wherever they surfaced, both within herself and in the systems she was a part of. Throughout the week, she also took note of her everyday interactions. At work, she noticed how quickly she made assumptions about a new colleague who was quiet during meetings—assuming they lacked confidence rather than considering that they might be facing systemic or cultural barriers.

Mira remembered a similar instance at her last job, where she had assumed that a colleague, Ravi, who spoke with a heavy accent, wasn't confident in his technical skills simply because he hesitated when speaking up. She hadn't realized at the time how her own cultural lens and biases had made her assume that fluency in English was equivalent to competence. She remembered noticing that Ravi was often overlooked or talked over during meetings—his ideas were appropriated by others who were more confident and fluent in their communication. She regretted not standing up for him sooner, not making space for his voice. Now, with her new awareness, she vowed to use her positionality to amplify voices like Ravi's rather than simply falling in line with the unspoken cultural norms of her workplace.

In another moment, she found herself feeling wary of a young man wearing a hoodie while walking behind her in the parking lot. As she paid attention to her body's initial unconscious reaction, she found herself gripping her purse handle tightly, and squeezing the bag against her torso with her elbow. She wondered what it felt like to be in a hoodie-wearing brown body who notices when people get nervous and protective around them. There's nothing inherently scary about hoodies or brown bodies, but the combination is a negative and harmful stereotype. She realized her reaction was shaped by societal stereotypes that she didn't consciously endorse but had absorbed over time.

Each instance made her more aware of the filters she used, and she wrote them down, reflecting on where they came from and how they influenced her behavior.

"One step at a time," she whispered to herself, echoing Elara's words. She knew this journey would be long, but she also knew it was worth taking.

CHAPTER 13

Expand Your Perspective
ELARA'S LESSON

Several weeks had passed, and Mira walked up the forest path leading to Elara's sanctuary, her eyes wandering over the vibrant greens of the leaves overhead and the golden light filtering through the branches. The forest felt alive, and each step seemed to echo the rhythm of her heart—steady, purposeful. She felt a deep sense of awe at the beauty around her—the sound of birds singing, the scent of damp earth, the way the sunlight danced across the forest floor. Moments like these reminded her of how interconnected everything was and how small yet significant her role could be in this vast world.

As she approached the sanctuary, she saw Elara standing at the entrance, her expression warm and inviting. Elara waved, and Mira felt a familiar sense of comfort wash over her like she was coming home after a long journey.

"Welcome back, Mira," Elara greeted her warmly. "I can see the joy in your eyes—you've been taking in the beauty of the forest."

Mira nodded, smiling softly. "It's hard not to. Everything feels so alive here."

Elara's smile widened. "That's good. It means you're present. Ready to begin today's work?"

Mira nodded, though she felt a slight pang of nervousness. "Yes, I think I am. What will we be doing?"

Elara smiled. "Today, we move into the second Perception practice—empathy-driven perspective-taking. We will explore how you see others and how they see you by focusing on empathy—the ability to fully understand someone else's experience by stepping outside your own lens."

Mira frowned slightly, trying to grasp the concept. She had learned about empathy before—how to be understanding and listen—but she wasn't sure how deeply she truly understood it. "How do I do that?" she asked.

Elara swept her palm downward, and the mirror began to ripple like pond. "The mirror will serve as a portal again today, Mira. You'll embody someone else, stepping into their world to experience life through their eyes and in their shoes.

Elara's tone shifted slightly, becoming more resolute. "Empathy isn't just about understanding someone's struggles, Mira," she added. "It's also about seeing their strengths, their unique contributions, and the value they bring. Too often, we approach people from a **deficit mindset**—focusing on what they lack or what makes them different. But to truly connect and create equity, we must adopt an **asset mindset**. This means recognizing people's skills, experiences, and perspectives as valuable assets rather than deficits and understanding how these can enrich our communities, workplaces, and relationships without reducing them to resources to be exploited."

Mira's brow furrowed, taking in Elara's words. The concept resonated with her. She recalled a recent nature-based STEM outreach event where she had hesitated to let a young girl lead a group activity because the girl's approach seemed unconventional. Mira had initially felt critical of the girl's method, worrying it might disrupt the lesson plan. But when she stepped back and allowed the girl to proceed, she realized that the young leader's creativity and unique perspective engaged the group more effectively than Mira's original plan. The experience had taught her the value of letting go of rigid expectations and recognizing different approaches as assets. This new understanding of an asset mindset felt daunting but also liberating as if it opened the door to seeing the world differently.

The mirror's surface shifted, capturing Mira's attention again. It began exuding a glowing liquid light. Mira took a deep breath, attempting to steady her quickening heart. Elara's words echoed in her mind: 'Trust the mirror.' Mira felt her nerves tighten, and then she exhaled.

As if sensing her readiness, the mirror's shimmering surface rippled outward. Suddenly, Mira felt herself pulled in, weightlessly floating into a new world. Opening her eyes, she found herself in a place unlike anything she had experienced before.

She was inhabiting the body of an older man—Guy. His body felt worn, weary, and tense. Mira felt an ache in his muscles, a rawness in his spirit, and a sense of heaviness in his entire being, a fatigue that seemed to seep into his bones. She was on a street corner, sitting against a rough brick wall, surrounded by the sounds of cars, people, and the occasional blare of a distant siren. Guy was an unhoused Vietnam veteran, and Mira could feel the constant buzz of unease in his mind—a side effect of the PTSD that had lingered with him for years.

Mira could feel the cold seeping through his clothes, the hunger gnawing at his stomach. She could also feel the impact of people's stares—some filled with pity, others with disgust, but most simply dismissive. They passed by as if Guy were invisible.

He held a small cardboard sign in his hand, the words scrawled in shaky letters: "Veteran in need of help." Mira felt the deep shame that Guy carried. He hadn't always been this way. He remembered when he was young, standing proudly in his uniform, serving his country. He remembered his friends, the camaraderie, the sense of purpose. But he also remembered the horrors he had seen—the screams, the loss, the chaos of war.

Guy's memories flashed through Mira's mind, fragmented and haunting. The explosions, the faces of friends who didn't make it back, the loneliness that consumed him when he returned home. Mira could feel the deep, invisible wounds of trauma—how they had cut Guy off from his family, from jobs, from stability. She felt his fear at night, the hyper-vigilance that never let him sleep peacefully, the feeling that he was always one step away from danger.

A woman walked by, her eyes catching his for a moment before looking away quickly. Mira felt Guy's heart sink further—he had grown used to that look, the way people couldn't bear to see him. They preferred that he remain unseen, as though his presence reminded them of something uncomfortable they'd rather forget. Mira could feel his isolation, the gnawing thought that he might not belong anywhere anymore.

But there were moments of light too—Guy's memories of his fellow veterans, the military brothers he still sometimes saw at the shelter, the way they shared stories, cigarettes, and sometimes laughter. He remembered a woman who worked at a local community center, who always offered him a hot meal without judgment. These small acts of kindness kept him going, making him feel like maybe, just maybe, he was still human, still worthy of dignity.

Mira felt Guy's pride, the slivers of resilience he held onto—the will to keep going even when the world seemed to have forgotten him. She felt the pull he faced between wanting to ask for help and the overwhelming burden of shame that made him want to disappear.

Then, just as suddenly as it had begun, the world around Mira started to dissolve. The colors blurred, and she felt herself being pulled back. Her senses shifted as she returned to her own body. She opened her eyes to find herself in Elara's sanctuary, the mirror's glow fading.

Mira gasped, her hands trembling. She felt the tears welling in her eyes. The wave of emotions—fear, pain, loneliness, and flickers of hope—rushed through her, leaving her breathless.

Elara watched her with compassionate eyes. "Take your time, Mira," she said softly.

Mira closed her eyes, tears slipping down her cheeks. "It was so much... the pain, the memories, the feeling of being so invisible." She looked up at Elara, her voice breaking. "I could feel how deeply he wanted to be seen, to be valued, but also the shame that held him back from asking for help."

Elara nodded. "It's a heavy burden to bear, the burden of invisibility. Empathy isn't about fixing—it's about truly seeing, about holding space for those experiences without judgment."

Mira took a deep breath, her voice trembling. "I think I'm beginning to grasp it now. I realize how easy it is to overlook someone like Guy, to forget that every person has a story, a past, pain, and hope. It's not just about feeling sorry for them—it's about recognizing their humanity."

Elara stepped closer, placing a hand on Mira's shoulder. "And that recognition, Mira, is the first step towards genuine empathy-driven action. It's about seeing and standing with others, even in small ways. This also requires understanding the harm of **dehumanization**—the process of stripping someone of their positive human qualities, often reducing them to objects or associating them with animals. When we fail to recognize someone's humanity, it becomes easier to dismiss their struggles or justify inequity. True empathy means rejecting dehumanization and affirming the full humanity of everyone we encounter."

Mira nodded, her heart aching but also feeling a flicker of resolve. She knew she couldn't change everything for someone like Guy, but she could change how she saw people like him. She could choose to see them, honor their experiences, and use her positionality to amplify their humanity rather than ignore it.

The shimmering mirror slowly transformed, and magically, Mira found herself in a completely different setting—a community center where people were gathered for an open discussion about neighborhood safety. She looked down and realized she was inhabiting the body of Malik, a middle-aged Black man sitting in a circle of chairs surrounded by people from his community. He had spoken up earlier, sharing concerns about the safety of his teenage sons walking home in the evenings.

Mira could feel Malik's nervousness—his voice wavered as he spoke, and his heart pounded as he worried about being judged and misunderstood. He wanted to protect his family, but he also didn't want to be seen as paranoid or as someone who was overreacting. As he spoke, a White woman across the circle responded, her tone dismissive. "I think you're exaggerating," she said. "This neighborhood is safe. I've lived here for years, and nothing has ever happened."

Mira could feel the sting of the words, the dismissal of his concerns. She wanted to argue, to defend Malik's perspective—but instead, she took a deep breath and tried to see it from the woman's point of view. She remembered Elara's guidance—"perspective-taking." Perhaps this woman had never experienced fear for her safety or her children's safety. Perhaps her lived experience had shielded her from understanding Malik's fears.

Mira felt the frustration mixed with empathy. She could see how Malik's identity—a Black father raising two teenage boys—

influenced his fears and his need to speak up. She could also see how the woman's positionality—perhaps as someone who had never faced racial profiling or systemic bias—affected her ability to understand his concerns and the very real dangers they faced by simply walking in their neighborhood.

"I understand that you feel safe here," Malik said, his voice steady, "but my experience has been different. I worry for my sons because I've seen what can happen. I hope we can work together to ensure everyone feels that same sense of safety."

Mira could feel the room shift slightly—not a complete change, but a softening. The woman's expression changed, her eyes widening slightly as she nodded. It wasn't about changing her mind entirely—it was about planting a seed of understanding, about opening the door to empathy.

The mirror flashed, and suddenly, Mira was back in her own body, standing in front of Elara, her breath shaky. She felt a wave of emotion—Guy's exhaustion, Malik's vulnerability, and their desire to be seen and understood.

Mira stood there momentarily, trying to process everything she had just felt. She was overwhelmed by the intensity of Guy's and Malik's experiences. Tears welled in her eyes, and she could not hold back the emotion built up during the journey.

Elara nodded, her eyes filled with empathy. "Empathy is not easy, Mira. It requires vulnerability. It requires letting go of your perspective and fully stepping into someone else's experience. It requires recognizing the emotions involved, staying out of judgment, and finding a way to connect."

Mira swallowed, her heart heavy. "I felt how hard it was. Not just to understand but to let go of my instinct to fix things or defend my viewpoint."

"That's the key," Elara said softly. "Empathy isn't about fixing. It's about being present and understanding that sometimes there is no solution—only connection. The mirror helps you see that empathy is about holding space for others, even when their reality is different from yours."

Mira continues, "As I embodied Malik and Guy, I could better understand their experiences. I wish that the people they interacted with could have done that. I can see now that part of understanding my positionality requires perspective-taking. My experiences as a White woman mean that I've rarely been questioned for being in spaces where I belong or having my intentions doubted. But others, like Malik and Guy, face systemic challenges that I have never had to consider. My positionality often shields me from seeing the hurdles they face. It allows me to see who I am in relation to others, and empathy is the bridge that allows that to happen. If the woman arguing with Malik had used perspective-taking, she might not have minimized Malik's very real fears for his sons. And if those who passed by Guy on the street had paused to consider his humanity—to imagine what led him to that corner—perhaps they could have seen the man behind the sign instead of just avoiding him."

"The accumulation of these events, sometimes called **microinequities, microaggressions**, or **microassaults**, add up. They are not isolated incidents but part of systemic patterns that devalue certain identities while privileging others. This accumulation is not without consequence—it leads to burnout, stress, and even withdrawal from exclusionary spaces. The burden is not just emotional; it's systemic." Elara adds. "We'll talk more about that in the future, but the takeaway for today is the value of empathy-driven perspective-taking."

Mira nodded, feeling a mix of exhaustion and clarity. "So, what do I do now?"

"You practice," Elara said, a soft smile playing on her lips. "In your daily life, invite others to share their perspectives. Listen without the need to solve. Use empathy as a bridge to understanding the impact of different experiences, systemic advantages, and disadvantages. And remember—it's a journey. One that takes time and requires you to move forward, one step at a time."

"What about times when I cannot ask someone their perspective?" Mira inquires.

"Great point, Mira. Perspective-taking doesn't require that you always KNOW their perspective. Perspective-taking is the ability to understand and consider the thoughts, feelings, and experiences of others. It involves seeing a situation from another person's point of view and understanding the context that shapes their reactions. It's not just about imagining their situation but also understanding the systems they are up against—the cultural, social, and institutional forces that influence how they experience the world. It's a key component of social behavior, especially when breaking down biases and misconceptions. Empathy, as you suggested, is your bridge. As you move through interactions, I want you to remember this tool: ask yourself, 'What else might be true?' before reacting or making judgments. It's a simple five-word statement. To make this strategy more tangible, use your hand to count five possible alternatives—mirroring the five words in the phrase. Imagine your hand expanding along with your mind, opening doors to new ideas while sidestepping the confines of biased thinking. This simple gesture prevents us from tumbling into costly rabbit holes of misconception. The question helps you broaden your perspective and practice empathy in real-time by consciously challenging your initial assumptions. It invites you to consider multiple possibilities, helping you shift away from a fixed viewpoint and reducing the risk of snap judgments or biases. Empathy-driven perspective-taking takes practice—especially when biases influence our initial reactions. Start small—whether in a work meeting, with family or even with strangers you encounter. The more you ask 'What else might be true?' you'll start to see beyond your initial lens and challenge the narratives you've internalized."

Mira took a deep breath and repeated, "What else might be true?" as the force of the lesson settled. She knew that this journey was far from over, but she also knew she was ready to take the next step—to practice empathy, open herself up, and see the world through a new lens.

CHAPTER 14

Expand Your Perspective
MIRA'S REFLECTION

The weeks following Mira's visit to Elara were different. The lesson on empathy-driven perspective-taking weighed heavily on her mind, and she knew she could not simply learn from it and move on. It was a practice, an ongoing journey of seeing the world through others' experiences, and each day presented an opportunity for her to try.

Mira sat at her work desk during lunch, her journal open before her, her pen resting on the page. At the top, she had written a single question: *"What else might be true?"* Below it, she had drawn five circles, each representing an alternative perspective. She stared at the blank page, the question echoing in her mind.

She reflected on her earlier interaction with her colleague, Jenna. During their team meeting, Jenna seemed curt, barely making eye contact and responding to questions with short, clipped answers. Mira's initial reaction was frustration. She wondered, *"Why is Jenna being so rude? Is she upset with me?"* The irritation simmered as the day went on, but Mira remembered her conversation with Elara. She took a deep breath and decided to use the tool Elara had given her.

Mira closed her eyes and thought, *What else might be true?* Slowly, she began to count the possibilities on her fingers:

1. Maybe Jenna was having a rough morning—perhaps she was tired or overwhelmed by something outside of work.
2. Maybe she felt unprepared for the meeting and was feeling insecure.
3. Maybe something in her personal life—a family issue or a health concern—was weighing on her mind.
4. Perhaps she didn't feel heard during previous meetings and had decided it wasn't worth engaging.
5. Maybe she was reacting to stress from the project timeline and wasn't aware of how it came across.

With each possibility, Mira felt her perspective expand. The irritation that had clouded her thoughts softened. Instead of assuming that Jenna was deliberately rude or that her behavior reflected Mira herself, she began to see Jenna as a person—someone with her own struggles and challenges, someone whose experience Mira could not fully know.

Later that afternoon, Mira decided to approach Jenna, not with frustration but with curiosity and care. She found her sitting in the break area, a coffee cup cradled in her hands. Mira took a deep breath and walked over.

"Hey, Jenna," Mira began gently. "You seemed a little distracted during the earlier meeting, and I just wanted to check-in. Is everything okay?"

Jenna looked up, her eyes softening as she met Mira's gaze. She sighed, a small, weary smile playing on her lips. "Thanks for asking, Mira. Honestly, it's been a tough morning. My mom's not recovering well from her surgery, and I guess I was distracted. I've recently taken on caregiving for her in my home, and the transition has been overwhelming and not particularly smooth.

I wasn't at my best this morning, and I didn't mean to come off as short."

Mira nodded, her heart warming with empathy. "I'm so sorry to hear about your mom not doing well and the challenging transition. Caregiving for an aging parent is a big responsibility, and I didn't know you were doing that. Thank you for sharing with me, Jenna. If there's anything I can do to help or if you need some space or just an ear to listen, please let me know."

Jenna's smile widened, a hint of gratitude in her eyes. "Thanks, Mira. That means a lot."

Mira walked away from the interaction, feeling the power of empathy-driven perspective-taking. It had transformed what could have been a day filled with resentment and misunderstanding into a moment of connection. Her parents were still healthy and independent, so she couldn't imagine taking on a responsibility like that right now. It was hard to imagine what Jenna was going through with little kids and an aging mom in her house.

Lately, her thoughts kept drifting back to Ruby—the friend who had shared her story in the coffee shop, whose pain Mira hadn't fully understood. She remembered how deeply she had wanted to connect, to understand. It was that desire, that drive to be a better friend, that had first led her to seek out Elara's guidance. She realized that true empathy wasn't about offering solutions but about being willing to sit in discomfort to recognize her own limitations in understanding. She wrote in her journal:

Today, I realized that perspective-taking is not just about understanding others—it's about actively choosing to see beyond my assumptions, to open myself up to the possibility that what I see is only one small part of a much larger picture.

She paused, her pen hovering above the page before adding:

Empathy-driven perspective-taking is not easy. It requires effort, vulnerability, and a willingness to be wrong about my initial assumptions—especially when those assumptions are shaped by my positionality and experiences. My background has given me certain advantages, but it also means I am challenged to understand what others face. It means asking, "What else might be true?" before reacting, and it means accepting that my perspective is limited. Today, I saw how my own positionality had initially led me to judge Jenna unfairly, to assume her behavior was about me when it wasn't.

Soon after, Mira attended a panel discussion at the IEEE Women in Engineering annual conference. The topic was workplace culture, and Mira was eager to learn from the speakers. As she entered the conference hall, her eyes landed on a familiar face—Brooke, her former colleague. Mira's mind flashed back to the resignation email Brooke had sent her months ago. Polite but direct, it had cut deeply: Brooke had found a new job with a culture that better suited her growth. Mira remembered the times during their one-on-ones when Brooke had tried to communicate her struggles, only for Mira to respond with platitudes like, "Stay optimistic." At the time, Mira had thought she was being supportive, but now she realized she had been dismissive, trying to slap positivity on a deeper wound. It was evident that Brooke was thriving in her new role as one of the featured panelists.

Mira's chest tightened. Brooke appeared poised and self-assured as she shared insights about creating supportive environments for growth. Mira couldn't help but compare herself, noticing the gaps in her own leadership style that Brooke's success seemed to highlight. At first, Mira felt defensive and hurt, her mind racing with excuses and justifications. But then she remembered Elara's lesson. *What else might be true?*

She took a deep breath and activated her empathy-driven perspective-taking. She considered Brooke's position and her own role in their shared history. Brooke's departure had been one of the moments that motivated Mira to begin this journey. She recognized how her positionality as a leader might have created gaps in understanding that affected Brooke's experience.

After the panel, Mira approached Brooke during the networking session. Brooke greeted her with a polite smile. "Mira, it's been a while."

"It has," Mira replied, her voice steady. "You were fantastic up there. I learned a lot. Thank you for sharing your experiences."

Brooke's expression softened slightly. "Thank you. You know, I'm grateful for the opportunities I had while working with you, though I'll admit there were challenges that led me to leave. But I guess you just heard about some of those. I probably could have saved you a front-row seat with a little heads-up about what to expect." Brooke chuckled, the sound carrying an awkward edge that mirrored Mira's own unease.

Mira's instinct was to respond defensively, but she caught herself. She took a deep breath, closing her eyes briefly to reset, choosing her words carefully. "I've been reflecting on that time a lot, actually. I'm sorry for the ways I failed as a leader. Hearing you today reminded me how important it is to truly listen and hear people when they express a need rather than shrugging it off with platitudes or overlooking the reality and nuance of their experience. It is important to intentionally create a culture where people can thrive."

Brooke's eyes flickered with surprise before she smiled. "Thank you, Mira. That means a lot to hear. I hope the work you're doing now brings positive change."

Mira walked away from the conversation with a mix of emotions: gratitude for Brooke's grace, sorrow for her past mistakes, and a renewed commitment to doing better. Yet, beneath the surface, she felt a wave of discomfort churn in her stomach. Hearing Brooke's candid acknowledgment of the challenges that led to her departure was like holding a mirror up to her own failings. Mira wanted to defend herself, to claim her good intentions, to explain how much she had tried. But she knew none of that would change the truth: her leadership had fallen short. The realization stung deeply, almost physically, and for a moment, it was hard to breathe.

She reflected on the tension within her, the raw vulnerability of confronting her mistakes so publicly. Brooke's poise contrasted sharply with Mira's inner turmoil, and that disparity only amplified the ache of regret. Still, Mira recognized that these feelings were part of her growth. Brooke's success reminded her that people could thrive in the right environment and underscored the importance of organizational culture. With that thought, she resolved to turn her discomfort into determination—a motivation to create spaces where her future employees wouldn't feel compelled to leave.

That night, Mira wrote in her journal:

Today, I saw the tangible impact of leadership decisions on an employee's well-being and growth. Brooke's story is a testament to the power of creating supportive environments. It's not only about patching personal relationships; it's about real change. I'm grateful for what I learned from her today and sorry for the ways I fell short. I'm committed to doing better.

Yet, I can't ignore the raw discomfort I felt. Listening to Brooke on that stage, knowing her words came from experiences I had contributed to, was like walking through fire. I wanted to defend myself, to interrupt and plead that my intentions were good. But the truth—cold, stark, and undeniable—was that good intentions weren't enough. Leadership isn't about what I meant to do; it's about what I actually did. And hearing the echoes of my failures laid bare, even if indirectly, felt like swallowing a stone.

I also realized how my positionality shaped my reactions. I've had the privilege of seeing challenges from a distance, of interpreting struggles through my own lens, often missing the nuances of others' lived experiences. Brooke's story reminded me that empathy-driven perspective-taking isn't just about understanding others; it's about understanding how Brooke's identity as a Black woman who uses a wheelchair added layers of complexity to her experience that I failed to fully see or even consider. Her resignation letter echoed the times during our one-on-ones when she tried to communicate her struggles, and I brushed them aside with well-meaning but dismissive platitudes. I thought I was being supportive, but I was imposing my perspective instead of truly listening. This isn't just about confronting my limitations but about expanding my perspective to truly understand others' experiences. It means challenging my assumptions, leaning into empathy, and consistently asking, "What else might be true?" to see their full reality through the lens of their identities.

Still, I have to remember Brooke's success isn't only a mirror for my shortcomings; it's a guidepost. It shows me that people can flourish when given the right environment and that knowledge fuels me. I'm determined to turn this unease into action, to do better for those I lead now and in the future.

Mira sighed, leaning back in her chair. She thought about how often she had moved through life without considering the context of others—how often she had seen others only through the filter of her own experiences and positionality. She knew that if she truly wanted to be a better friend, neighbor, and leader, she had to understand others, too. And that meant practicing empathy, stepping out of her own lens, and being open to the realities of those around her.

Mira turned the page in her journal, jotting down a reminder for herself:

Perspective-taking is an intentional shift—a choice to see differently. My positionality shapes my view, but empathy allows me to expand it. Keep asking: What else might be true?

The interim between visits had not been without its challenges. There were moments when Mira found herself slipping back into old habits—judging quickly, assuming she understood a situation at face value. But each time, she caught herself. She paused, asked the question, and practiced shifting her perspective. It was tiring, and it took effort, but it also felt right. It felt like growth.

Mira thought about what Elara had said—that empathy was about holding space for others, even when their reality was different from her own. It was about bridging the gap that her positionality created, about seeing beyond her own experience. With each passing day, she felt herself getting better at it—one small step at a time.

She smiled softly to herself, her pen resting on the final line of the page. She knew this journey of empathy-driven perspective-taking was only beginning, and she was ready to keep moving forward.

She wrote, *Next week, I'll return to Elara, ready to continue this journey—not because it's always easy or rewarding, but because it's necessary. It's hard, exhausting, and often frustrating, yet it's also where growth happens, where new perspectives emerge, and where change begins. I'll go back ready to learn, to stumble, to grow, and to see the world through a new and expanded lens.*

CHAPTER 15

See Beyond Yourself
ELARA'S LESSON

Mira returned to Elara's sanctuary, reflecting on the empathy-driven perspective-taking she had practiced. The last phase had shown her the importance of stepping outside her own lens, and she felt ready to continue the journey. Today, she was eager to delve deeper into the complexities of perception.

Elara greeted Mira warmly, her eyes filled with understanding. She motioned toward the glowing mirror, its energy gently pulsing as if it were alive. Mira felt a sense of anticipation in the air.

"Today, Mira, we move to the final practice of the **Perception** phase," Elara began, her tone wrapped in quiet reassurance. "This practice is about understanding how others perceive you—but recognizing that these perceptions may not always be based on your actions. Instead, they might be influenced by broader systemic mistrust or accumulated past hurt or harm experiences."

Mira nodded, intrigued. She thought back to her friend Ruby—the conversation that had first brought her to Elara. She had often wondered how her actions were received, especially by those closest to her. She had never considered that their reactions could be influenced by layers of past experiences she might never fully understand.

"The mirror will once again be a portal," Elara said as she motioned subtly, and the mirror flickered to life. Today, you will step into the lives of three individuals, each with a unique story. By experiencing life through their eyes, you will understand that people's perceptions of others may not always be based on their actions but rather on past experiences. I want you to notice what Jaz, Ben, and Sam are feeling and perceiving about the characters opposite of them in their scenarios."

Mira took a deep breath and nodded. "Ok, let's do it," she whispered, closing her eyes as she stepped forward, feeling the familiar pull of the mirror. When she opened her eyes, she found herself in a carefully crafted bedroom. The serene green walls were covered in photography and homemade abstract nature paintings, and the relaxing bed was hugged by a flowy canopy with greenery and twinkling lights. She looked down at her hands—smaller, younger, with chipped red nail polish. Mira was now in the body of Jaz, a mixed-race sixteen-year-old foster kid who had clearly been through a lot. The room around her was a testament to the foster mom's efforts—carefully designed from a curated Pinterest board Jaz had once shared. It was meant to be the room of Jaz's dreams, crafted with the hope of making her feel at home and loved, especially as adoption was the ultimate goal. But Mira could feel the lingering doubt, the refusal to trust or believe in such gestures, shaped by all of Jaz's previous experiences.

The door opened, and in walked a woman—a new foster mom in her early forties. Her demeanor was relaxed and composed. She wore a warm smile, and a gentleness in her eyes suggested she was trying to connect.

The foster mom spoke softly to Jaz, her voice calm and caring. "I just wanted to see if you were okay. I know this must be hard for you. I heard about what happened at school, and I'm here to help."

Jaz crossed her arms defensively, her eyes narrowing at the foster mom. Even the effort she'd put into crafting the perfect room felt suspect to Jaz, a reminder of promises that always seemed too good to be true. There was a wall of mistrust—a sense that no matter what this woman said, it couldn't be trusted. The idea of adoption, of permanence, felt like another unreachable promise Jaz couldn't let herself believe in. It wasn't that the foster mom was doing anything wrong—Jaz could feel her genuine care—but it didn't matter. Jaz yelled, "You are just another dumb White lady who wants to save a poor little Black kid!" The foster mom gasped, visibly hurt. Jaz had been let down too many times before by adults who had promised to be there and then disappeared. This was her protective mechanism—a learned instinct to distrust to avoid further pain. The foster mom's efforts to connect were probably genuine, but Jaz's resistance wasn't about her—it was about all the adults before who had broken their promises.

Suddenly, Mira was pulled from the room, the scene fading as she felt herself transported once more. She opened her eyes in a busy office environment, looking down at broad, masculine hands. She was now in the body of Ben, a Black man in his early thirties, dressed professionally and sitting at a meeting table surrounded by colleagues.

A woman entered the room, speaking energetically as she handed out documents. She was the new team lead—assertive and confident, commanding the group's attention. Mira felt a tension rise in Ben's chest—a skepticism and guardedness that wouldn't go away. It wasn't anything the team lead had done specifically, but Ben had been in too many meetings where his contributions were brushed aside because of his skin color. The dynamics weren't personal; they were shaped by systemic biases that had long existed. He assumed this woman—a White woman in authority—would dismiss or underestimate him, just like others before.

Mira sensed how Ben held back, unwilling to fully engage. The team lead's confidence could easily be misinterpreted as dismissiveness, her directness as arrogance—especially by someone who had been repeatedly marginalized. The history of power dynamics influenced how every action was perceived, adding tension to even the simplest interactions.

Suddenly, Mira felt the world shift again, and when she opened her eyes, she found herself in a new scenario. She looked down at her hands—slimmer, with fingertips nervously tapping against her pants. She was now in the body of Sam, a young **neurodivergent non-binary** person in their early twenties, sitting in a crowded classroom.

Mira felt anxiety welling up—their senses were on overdrive. The lights were too bright, the scribbling of pens grated against their ears, and the ticking clock seemed unbearably loud. Sam's chest tightened, and their breathing grew shallow. The professor called their name, echoing through the room, and Mira panicked. They wanted to answer, but their thoughts were jumbled, and the words refused to come out.

The professor stood at the front, waiting. She looked patient, but the gaze of the professor, along with Sam's peers, felt like a spotlight. Mira felt small and misunderstood, aware that others might think she, as Sam, wasn't paying attention or, worse, that she didn't care. It wasn't that the professor was unkind—her patience was evident—but the environment was overwhelming and suffocating. Mira assumed the professor, like others before, thought Sam wasn't trying hard enough. It wasn't malice but a lack of understanding of what it was like to navigate the world with a neurodivergent mind.

Mira could feel how Sam's neurodivergence made simple things—like being called upon to answer a question—feel overwhelming. She saw how Sam's hesitance might be perceived as disinterest or lack of effort when, in reality, the struggle to filter out the noise, the lights, and the multitude of stimuli made it difficult to focus.

Then, just as suddenly as before, the scene dissolved, and Mira found herself back in Elara's sanctuary. Her heart felt heavy, her thoughts swirling with the complexity of what she had just experienced.

Elara looked at her kindly, nodding. "It is difficult, isn't it?" she said softly. "To realize that how others perceive us is often shaped by systems, structures, and histories beyond our control. Consider how the people interacting with Jaz, Ben, and Sam might have responded differently. With empathy, they could have been kind and considerate, but without it, they might have become defensive, causing harm rather than building connection. Staying grounded in empathy helps us avoid defensiveness and create genuine understanding."

Mira swallowed, her voice barely a whisper. "It's hard to accept that someone might see me as part of the problem, even when I'm trying not to be."

Elara stepped closer, her gaze steady. "It's challenging to see the systems when they were built to benefit you. Without experiencing the same barriers, it's easy to overlook the obstacles others face. But now, you are beginning to see those barriers, Mira. Understanding that others' reactions aren't always personal is what will help you become a better ally, leader, and person."

Mira nodded slowly, tears welling in her eyes. "My identity—the privileges I hold—shapes how others perceive me. Their reactions come from a lifetime of experiences that often have nothing to do with me personally. But if I stay open and approach them with empathy, I might be able to help break down some of those barriers."

Elara smiled warmly. "Exactly, Mira. Your homework this week is to reflect on how others might perceive you—not based on your intentions, but on their lived experiences. Use the tools you've learned: empathy, perspective-taking, and the understanding that perception, while not always accurate, can still be someone's reality as a form of self-protection."

"I will," Mira said quietly, compassion coursing through her. "I'll do my best to stay open, to understand, and to connect—even when it's hard."

Elara's smile widened. "That's all any of us can do, Mira. Treat people with kindness, dignity, and respect. By doing so, you build trust, one interaction at a time. The journey continues, and you are growing with every step."

CHAPTER 16

See Beyond Yourself
MIRA'S REFLECTION

Mira sat in her favorite corner of the coffee shop, her journal open in front of her. She took a deep breath, tapping her pen against the edge of the page, the conversation with Elara replaying in her mind. She could still hear Elara's soothing voice, explaining that how others saw her could possibly have more to do with their own experiences than anything she had done. It was a challenging idea, one that felt deeply uncomfortable yet profoundly eye-opening. She wanted to extend more grace, kindness, and empathy to others.

In the back of her mind, she thought about her friend Ruby, who had shared her frustrations weeks earlier. Ruby had spoken candidly about the harm White people at work or in her life had caused her. Mira wondered what it would feel like to hear such conversations and not take them personally. She wanted to be the kind of friend who could truly understand—to listen without defensiveness, to see beyond herself, and to connect with empathy and respect. She reminded herself of the lesson from Elara: others' reactions are often shaped by their own experiences and struggles, not by her personally. This awareness encouraged Mira to observe how people responded to her, not as evidence of her own behavior but as a window into their lived experiences.

The chance to put Elara's lesson into practice came sooner than she expected. As she was waiting for her coffee, she noticed the barista, a young woman, looked visibly tense when it was Mira's turn. The barista's smile seemed forced, and her eyes darted nervously as she took Mira's order. Her words were curt, and her attitude was borderline rude. Mira felt a pang of defensiveness at first—did she do something wrong?

But then she remembered Elara's words, and she paused, taking a deep breath. "What else might be true?" she whispered to herself, letting the question settle into her mind as she watched the barista carefully prepare her drink.

Maybe she had a difficult customer before Mira, or maybe Mira reminded her of someone who had treated her poorly in the past. Maybe she was dealing with something completely unrelated, something heavy that had nothing to do with the people in front of her. The thought eased Mira's defensiveness. She took her drink with a sincere smile, and as she turned away, she offered a kind and genuine encouragement: "I hope your day gets better soon. I know it can be tough sometimes."

The barista's eyes widened slightly, and for the first time, her expression softened. She met Mira's eyes and gave a half smile, nodding slightly. "Thanks. I appreciate that."

Mira left the shop, feeling a small sense of fulfillment—not because she had solved the barista's problem, whatever it might have been, but because she had chosen to respond with kindness and empathy rather than defensiveness. It was a small shift, but it felt powerful. She realized that her default reactions were changing, that she was beginning to see herself and others through a new lens—one less shaped by her own need for affirmation and more by a desire for connection.

Later that week, Mira met with a new colleague, Alex, who had recently joined her team. She had heard murmurs around the office—Alex had a reputation for being difficult and distant. Mira remembered a similar experience from her own past, working on an engineering team at the beginning of her career. It had been a young, mostly male team that bonded over sports, beer, and toxic '**bro culture.**' Mira participated in an effort to fit in, and thus became complicit in the culture. She remembered a colleague, Brad, who had never participated in these activities, which, at the time, she had misinterpreted as unfriendliness. Only later did she learn that Brad was gay, and the homophobic banter and exclusionary culture had kept him away. Mira now saw how her assumptions and the atmosphere around her had influenced her perception of Brad. With this memory in mind, she realized Alex might be experiencing something similar. She knew she wanted to approach Alex with an open mind, understanding that the barriers between them could have more to do with the environment than with his personality. She sat across from him, watching as he carefully adjusted his notes, his expression guarded.

'*What else might be true?*' she asked herself silently. She remembered Elara's lessons, which reminded her that people's reactions often stemmed from past experiences. Maybe Alex's hesitation came from feeling out of place, from being new and trying to fit in. Maybe he had been in environments before where vulnerability was taken advantage of, where being guarded was safer than being open.

As they began the conversation, Mira leaned in, her tone considerate and open. "I know it's always a bit overwhelming to join a new team," she said, her smile soft. "It's a lot of new faces, new dynamics. I remember how it felt when I started here—it took me ages to feel comfortable."

Alex looked up, his guarded expression loosening. He blinked a few times before offering a small smile. "Yeah, it's... it's a lot," he admitted, his shoulders relaxing slightly. "I guess I'm still trying to figure out how I fit in."

Mira nodded, feeling the connection between them begin to form. She didn't push, didn't try to force more conversation, but let Alex set the pace, offering her understanding without expectation. By the end of the meeting, she noticed a difference in his demeanor—a slight ease that hadn't been there before.

As their relationship developed, Mira learned more about Alex's experience. He had joined the team with high hopes but quickly found himself alienated by the dominant culture. The offhand comments, the jokes at the expense of those who didn't fit the mold—these had built walls around Alex. Mira realized that her previous assumptions, influenced by office gossip, had overlooked the true reasons behind Alex's demeanor. It wasn't that he was unfriendly; it was that he was protecting himself in an environment that didn't feel safe.

Mira knew she couldn't change the culture of her team overnight, but she could take accountability for the team's current environment and her past carelessness in not paying closer attention to it. She could choose to approach Alex with understanding and offer grace instead of judgment. By fostering trust, showing empathy, and committing to doing better, she could contribute to building a team culture that prioritized **psychological safety** and **belonging**. And maybe, just maybe, she could start shifting the dynamics around her.

That evening, Mira sat down with her journal, reflecting on her day. She wrote about the barista from a few days earlier and about Alex, about how different it felt to approach these interactions without the need for validation, without defensiveness. She thought back to Elara's words: *Perception may not always be a reality, but it can still be someone else's reality—a reality shaped by their experiences, by systemic inequalities, and by the social norms that have either uplifted or constrained them.* She realized that many of the barriers others faced were not about individual actions alone but were deeply embedded in societal power dynamics.

Mira realized that part of her work in perception was learning to accept that others' responses to her might be influenced by things far beyond her control—by pain, fear, or mistrust that had nothing to do with her. Her role, then, was not to take it personally but to choose how she responded in those moments.

Mira recognized that accountability is crucial because mistakes and missteps are inevitable. As her social consciousness grew, she learned more about the experiences of others, and with that knowledge came a responsibility to respond. Without accountability, she knew she would fail to respect the dignity of those she wanted to support and might unintentionally cause harm. Mira realized that it wasn't enough to have good intentions; she needed to acknowledge when she got things wrong and model accountability. Too often, people deflect by claiming 'good intent.' But it was essential to remember: respect, don't deflect.

I'm learning to let go of the need to defend myself, she wrote, her pen moving slowly across the page. *Instead, I'm trying to be open, see others with empathy, and understand that their reactions are not always about me. When reactions are about me, I need to be self-aware enough to notice and then take accountability. Essentially, it's meeting people where they are, and maybe, just maybe, creating a space where they can feel seen and heard without fear.*

Mira looked at her words, a sense of peace settling over her. She knew this was part of her ongoing journey, but she felt ready for it—ready to move forward, one empathetic step at a time.

POSITIONALITY PRISM PART 3
Power

CHAPTER 17

Recognize Your Power
ELARA'S LESSON

Mira arrived at the sanctuary, her thoughts still circling around the lessons of perception she had practiced over the last several weeks. She remembered the promise she had made to herself—to become a better friend and community member and use what she was learning to lift others. The sanctuary seemed to echo her progress and honor her struggle, its glow richer and more focused, the air carrying a quiet intensity. The glowing mirror, more vibrant than before, seemed to anticipate the next step in her journey. Elara stood beside it, her expression kind and welcoming, her presence steady as always, yet with a glimmer of expectation that hinted at the importance of what was to come.

"Welcome back, Mira," Elara greeted her, signaling for Mira to take her usual seat. "You've done tremendous work on understanding **Personhood** and **Perception**—your identity and perspectives. Today, we begin the journey of understanding **Power**, the final piece of the **Positionality Prism**."

Mira sat down, her eyes glancing at the mirror that had become both a portal and a guide throughout her journey. "Power," she repeated thoughtfully. "It sounds heavy... and honestly, a little intimidating."

Elara smiled, nodding in understanding. "It can feel that way. But power itself is neither good nor bad. It's about how you use it. Understanding your power is an essential part of understanding your positionality. Today, we will explore where your power comes from, how it manifests, and the privileges that give you access in ways others might not have."

Mira shifted slightly, a mixture of curiosity and discomfort welling up inside her. "How do I even begin to think about my power? I don't really see myself as powerful."

Elara extended her hand toward the mirror, and the golden frame pulsed with quiet, commanding energy. The surface rippled, revealing a kaleidoscope of shifting images. Mira's reflection intertwined with fragments of her life—moments of confidence, hesitation, and influence. As she gazed, the mirror projected a vibrant scene where her decisions shaped outcomes for her team. It seemed to invite her to observe, engage, and recognize the threads of power woven through her everyday actions. The surface rippled, then shimmered with a radiant glow, drawing from an unseen source of strength. Slowly, an image materialized—a scene from Mira's life. She saw herself in a meeting at work, her voice clear and steady as she led a discussion. Her colleagues leaned in, listening attentively, her words shaping the group's direction. Mira watched, a flicker of uncertainty in her eyes as though trying to reconcile the authority she wielded with the weight of its responsibility.

"This is you," Elara said softly. "In this space, you hold power. You have a position of authority, your voice carries significance, and people look to you for direction. This power may not always feel like a grand, overwhelming force, but it shapes how others respond to you."

Mira nodded slowly. Seeing herself from the outside gave her a new perspective. She remembered that meeting—how easily people agreed with her ideas, how confident she had felt. But she also remembered the times she had seen others struggle to have their voices heard, particularly her quieter colleagues.

The mirror shifted again, showing Mira in a different setting—a community event, where she stood talking with some neighbors. She was smiling and engaging, and others were gathered around her, listening. Mira watched, a bit surprised. She had never thought of herself as a community leader, but there she was—influencing others and making decisions that impacted her neighborhood.

Elara turned to Mira, her voice gentle. "Power isn't only about having a big title or an important job. It's also about being able to influence people, having access to things others might not, and being in a position to help make decisions. Sometimes, it's obvious, like being the leader of a meeting, and other times, it's subtle—like having the **social capital** or **cultural wealth** that makes people turn to you for advice or direction. Recognizing this is the first step."

"Social capital?" Mira asked, her brow furrowing slightly.

Elara smiled, nodding. "**Social capital** means the people you know and the relationships you have that can help you get opportunities or make things happen. According to Dr. Tara Yosso's Model of Cultural Wealth, social capital encompasses the networks and support systems that help individuals navigate and thrive within various systems, particularly those that might otherwise marginalize them. It's a form of power rooted in community and mutual assistance, emphasizing collective strength over individual gain."

She paused, then continued, "**Cultural capital**, as Yosso defines it, is not about fitting into dominant cultural norms but about the assets and strengths rooted in one's community and experiences. This includes storytelling, linguistic skills, familial wisdom, and resistance to systemic inequities. It challenges the idea that only certain types of knowledge or behaviors are valuable, showing instead that cultural wealth is diverse and deeply empowering."

Mira swallowed her thoughts, a mix of introspection and unease. "I never thought about it that way. I always felt like I was just doing my part. I didn't think of it as having power."

Elara gave her a knowing smile. "Most people don't. Power can be easy to overlook, especially when you aren't accustomed to thinking of yourself in those terms. But with power comes responsibility—the responsibility to understand how you might use it to create equitable change and how your privileges have shaped your opportunities."

The mirror shimmered again, this time revealing moments from Mira's past—her school days, where teachers praised her work, and her university years when scholarships and mentors helped pave her path. Mira watched her younger self, a sense of pride mixed with the realization of how much support she had received along the way. She saw the ways her race, her upbringing, and her education had created opportunities that others might not have had.

"Privilege isn't about feeling guilty," Elara continued, her words laced with care. "It's about understanding where you fit into the larger picture. Recognizing your advantages—whether earned, given or simply part of your identity—helps you understand your positionality. Your race, your socioeconomic status, your education—these are all parts of what shapes your experiences and the power you have in the world. When you acknowledge your privilege, you begin to understand the ways in which you have power. Privilege provides unearned advantages, and these advantages can grant you influence and opportunities that others may not have. Privilege can also mean the absence of barriers faced by others. Recognizing the connection helps you see that privilege is a source of power, whether that power manifests in your ability to speak up without fear, be given the benefit of the doubt, or access opportunities others cannot, or with greater ease. And that awareness is what allows you to use your power to lift others."

Mira looked at Elara thoughtfully. "Can you give me some specific examples of what you mean? How do these privileges show up in real life?"

Elara nodded. "Of course, Mira. Let's consider a few situations." The mirror flashed, casting vibrant scenes behind Elara. Each scene aligned with her words: a classroom where Mira received a scholarship, a meeting where her guidance shaped a project's outcome and a neighborhood event where her voice led to collective action. The images danced, offering visual anchors to Elara's explanations. "Take your education, for instance. The mentors who guided you and the scholarships you received are examples of resources that contributed to your success. These systems and supports, while beneficial to you, are not accessible to everyone. Recognizing that these privileges afforded you influence and opportunities highlights one source of your power—access to resources. Social capital plays a role here as well. The connections and relationships you cultivated, such as friends and family who could offer advice or link you to internships, provided you with tools to navigate and thrive. This is how power can manifest, through access and opportunity."

She continued, "Another example is how you can move through public spaces without worrying about being stopped or questioned because of your race. You probably don't think about it much, but that's power and privilege—a lack of barriers that others, particularly people of color, face frequently. It grants you ease and safety that isn't shared by everyone."

Elara paused, watching Mira's expression shift as she considered these examples. "And think about your career. You have a network of connections—colleagues who respect you and people who value your ideas. This network, this social capital, gives you power. It means that you have people to turn to when you need support. For many, particularly those who are marginalized, building that network is a much steeper climb."

Mira acknowledged. "I see what you mean. It's not just about the obvious things—it's about the things I might not even notice because they've always been there for me. It's like there are layers—like understanding myself is the first layer, and then understanding how I fit into the world is another. Now, it's understanding what I can do with all of that."

Elara smiled. "Precisely, Mira. Today, I want you to expand on the list of advantages you began earlier after your third visit. Focus on how these advantages manifest in small, everyday moments—like speaking without interruption or having a network you can rely on for support. Reflect on how these privileges grant you power, whether through influence, access, or the ability to shape outcomes more easily than others. Consider how these privileges have minimized barriers in your life and contributed to your journey. There's no need for guilt—just awareness. And once you've recognized these privileges, think about how you might have used this power unconsciously in the past and how you can now use it intentionally to uplift and empower others."

Mira took a deep breath, her mind already turning to the task ahead. "It's about being intentional, isn't it? Recognizing what I have and figuring out how to share it."

"Exactly," Elara said. "This is the beginning of understanding power—not just as something you hold, but as something you can wield for good to create spaces that are more inclusive and equitable. It starts with awareness, and it grows with action."

Mira reached out to touch the glowing mirror, her fingers grazing its shimmering surface. The glass rippled under her touch, revealing a new scene. This time, she saw herself standing beside a colleague, offering guidance and support. Her words brought clarity to a complex problem, and her colleague's gratitude was evident. Mira's breath hitched as she realized the subtle ways her influence had made a difference. The mirror pulsed warmly as if affirming her growing understanding. A sense of bravery and determination settled within her as she resolved to wield her power and privilege with purpose. This journey was not just about understanding herself anymore—it was about what she could do for others. About how her own power, when used with intention, could help lift those around her.

"I'm ready," she whispered, her voice steady. "I want to understand my power so I can use it for good."

Mira turned back to the glowing mirror, her reflection steady and vibrant with color. She touched its surface, feeling a faint warmth, a hum of energy that seemed to connect her to the world around her. For the first time, she felt the weight and presence of her own power—reflected back at her in the mirror. It was not something external or overwhelming but an inherent part of her, waiting to be recognized. This moment of clarity revealed that power was not about what she did not yet understand but about seeing herself fully in relation to the world around her. "I'll start here," she thought as she smiled at her reflection, her resolve solidifying as the mirror pulsed gently, affirming her readiness.

CHAPTER 18

Recognize Your Power
MIRA'S REFLECTION

Mira stood at the door of her house, looking out into the world. Today, she decided, wouldn't be spent simply reflecting from her kitchen table. Today, she needed to actively observe her power—to notice it in action and see how it influenced her interactions with those around her.

She picked up her bag, slipped her journal inside, and headed out. As she walked through her neighborhood, she focused on moments of interaction, looking for signs of her power in each situation.

Mira visited a local florist she hadn't been to before. As she waited for the shopkeeper to arrange her bouquet, she noticed a young apprentice struggling to tie a ribbon. Mira smiled and said warmly to the shopkeeper, "It looks like you're doing a great job mentoring." The shopkeeper beamed, and the apprentice glanced up, visibly encouraged. Mira realized that even something as simple as positive reinforcement could be a form of power—an influence to uplift and support someone else's growth. She wrote a quick note in her journal while she sat with her coffee: *Power shows up in our attitude, in how we choose to use our words to inspire and make others feel valued.*

Reflecting on this interaction, Mira thought about her positionality—how her comfort in giving encouragement without fear of it being misconstrued was partly due to her identity. As a White woman in a familiar environment, she had the privilege of her words being trusted and received positively. This privilege made it easier for her to exert influence without fear of negative repercussions.

Next, Mira walked to her office building. People greeted her warmly as she entered, their faces lighting up at her arrival. She realized that her role at work gave her a certain presence—people saw her as someone who could influence decisions, someone whose voice mattered. She pulled out her phone and started a voice memo: "My title gives me influence. But do I always use that influence to benefit the group? Or do I just take it for granted?"

As she moved through the hallways, she continued recording her thoughts. "Would I be treated this way if I were someone else? If I were a woman of color, or a new hire, or someone without my title?" She paused, her voice softening. "My professional identity carries privileges that translate into power—power others might not have. How often do I recognize that? And am I using it to open doors for others or just for myself?"

She considered the weight of her words as she walked. Influence was not inherently neutral; it could uplift and empower, but it could also become a tool for self-interest or, worse, a source of harm. Her power in the workplace carried responsibility—every decision she made, every interaction she had, could shape someone else's experience.

Mira resolved to revisit these reflections later, knowing they held the key to her commitment to becoming a more inclusive and intentional leader. As she slipped her phone back into her bag, she thought, *It's not just about holding power—it's about how I choose to wield it.*

Later, during a meeting, Mira noticed how easily she could jump into the conversation and how the room seemed to give her space without hesitation—a big shift from earlier in her career. She decided to stay quiet for a few moments, observing instead. She noticed that when one of her quieter colleagues, Priya, tried to speak, she was often talked over. Mira stepped in, saying, "Let's hear what Priya has to say," and watched as the room refocused on her colleague. It was a small action, but Mira could feel the power she had to shape the flow of the conversation. Afterward, she wrote: *Power is about creating space for others, to amplify voices that might otherwise be lost or otherwise ignored.*

Mira also recognized that her ability to step in for Priya came from her privilege in the room. As someone whose voice was often heard, she had the power to ensure others were heard too. She realized that in her experience as a woman in engineering, she had often wished to not be talked over or for someone to step in for her. Now, her position allowed her to be that advocate for others.

That evening, Mira attended a planning meeting at her local community center. She noticed Victoria, a new resident, sitting near the back, not engaging with anyone. Mira thought about how easily she could join a conversation—how her familiarity with the community gave her confidence that Victoria didn't yet have. Mira approached Victoria, inviting her to join her table. Introducing Victoria to the group, Mira realized that her social and cultural capital—her comfort, connections, and status in the community—was another form of power. She had the ability to help someone feel included. Her comfort was a privilege that allowed her to extend a hand to someone else.

After the meeting, Mira took a moment to write in her journal while sitting on a bench outside: *Social and cultural capital is power. It gives me the ability to help create spaces where people can experience feelings of belongingness. I can use this to uplift others.*

On her walk home, Mira passed by a neighborhood playground. She saw a group of children playing and noticed one child sitting alone on the swings, watching the others. Mira recognized the longing in his eyes—he wanted to join but seemed hesitant. She approached one of the parents standing nearby who she knew, though not well, and struck up a conversation to mention the child on the swing. The parent noticed and walked over to invite the child to play. Mira watched as the boy's face lit up, and she realized that even when not directly in control, she could influence outcomes by noticing what others might not. She wrote: *Power isn't always direct. Sometimes it's about seeing what others miss and nudging them to act.*

Reflecting on this, Mira realized that her positionality allowed her to notice and act without fear. She had the privilege of being perceived as approachable, as someone whose intervention would be welcomed. She recognized that for others, perhaps someone who holds marginalized identities, this might have been more challenging.

By the time Mira returned home, she felt a deep sense of introspection and self-awareness—not just about the power she held but about how it appeared in small, everyday moments. She wrote in her journal: *Power is everywhere—in how we speak, how we listen, how we include others, and how we notice those on the margins. It's in the small choices, in the moments when we decide to act or stay silent.*

She paused, then added: *Privilege gives me power. Power gives me the ability to create change. And change starts with intention.*

Mira knew she still had much to learn, but for the first time, she felt she was beginning to understand how to use what she had—not just for herself, but for those around her. She closed her journal, feeling a renewed sense of purpose. She was ready to continue this journey, to keep learning, reflecting, and growing.

She added a final note: *This week, pay attention to where power shows up. Notice it in yourself, in others, in small moments, and in bigger contexts. Ask yourself—how can I use my power to create space and opportunities for those who might not have it?*

CHAPTER 19

Share Power

ELARA'S LESSON

Mira stepped into Elara's sanctuary, though this time, the feeling of readiness she usually carried was tinged with doubt. The previous visit had been eye-opening; she had begun to truly understand her power—how it showed up, how it influenced those around her, and how it was woven with privilege. But today, she also felt the weight of uncertainty, the nagging thought that maybe she wasn't ready at all. After all, doing the work to share power wasn't always graceful or easy. She had stumbled before, and the prospect of stumbling again loomed large. Still, she felt a pull toward something more—an urge to try, even if it wasn't perfect.

Elara greeted her with a warm smile, standing near the shimmering mirror. This time, the mirror's energy felt different—less pulsating and more like a tranquil, steady glow. It reminded Mira of a lake at dawn, brimming with quiet potential.

"Mira, welcome back," Elara began. "Today, we move forward on our journey together. You've been learning about your power—recognizing it, seeing how it shows up, and how privilege is intertwined with it. Now, it's time to take the next step: learning how to share that power."

Mira nodded, feeling the weight of Elara's words. "How do I share it?" she asked, curiosity mixing with uncertainty. "I understand that I have power, but how do I make sure I'm not just holding onto it?"

Elara smiled knowingly, pressed lightly on the frame, and the mirror revealed its shifting depths. "Sharing power is about creating space for others, Mira. It's about recognizing when it's your turn to step back so someone else can step forward. Today, the mirror will help you understand this practice by allowing you to embody those sharing their power."

Mira took a deep breath, feeling the energy of the moment. She closed her eyes as Elara spoke softly, "Trust the mirror, Mira. Let it show you what it means to share power, to make space for others."

The familiar warmth enveloped her, and Mira felt herself being pulled forward into the shimmering depths of the mirror. When she opened her eyes again, she found herself embodying a soldier, Aaron, who was in uniform and invited to speak on a panel about mental health. Mira felt his confidence but also a hesitation as he asked the event organizer a simple question: "Who are the other panelists?" As the organizer listed the names of well-known military personnel, it became clear—it was a "manel," an all-male panel. Aaron took a deep breath, and Mira could feel the decision being made. With a sense of purpose, he spoke. "Thank you for the invitation," he said, "but I think it would be more impactful if you included diverse perspectives. Let me suggest a fellow soldier—a woman who has great experience and insight to share."

The scene shifted, and Mira now found herself inhabiting another person—this time, a keynote speaker, Tascha, invited to a multi-day conference. She could feel pride in being invited, but she also had an awareness of her privilege as a person with lighter skin. Mira—now in Tascha's body—requested her speaking fee but added an important note: "I want to ensure that all keynote speakers receive the same rate, regardless of identity. Please confirm that there will be parity among us." The organizer hesitated, visibly taken aback by the request, but eventually nodded in agreement. Mira felt the power of not just accepting what was offered but questioning it to make space for fairness and equity for others who might otherwise be undervalued.

Suddenly, her perspective shifted. Mira now inhabited Phil, a community leader respected for his insights and experience. She felt a different kind of influence—the ease with which the group seemed to accommodate Phil's voice. The adults around her were discussing high schoolers, their habits, challenges, and how best to support them. The conversation was lively, but something was missing.

Phil noticed Ethan, a high school junior who had been quietly listening from the edge of the circle. His expression was thoughtful, but he hadn't said a word. Mira knew what it was like to be in that position—surrounded by adults speaking about you, but not to you. She felt a pang of recognition, remembering her own experiences of wanting to be heard but not knowing how to jump in.

Phil decided to make a different choice. Clearing his throat, he said, "Ethan, you've got a unique perspective here that we might be missing. I'd love to hear what you think about all this."

The conversation paused, and all eyes turned to Ethan. Mira felt the deliberate act of creating space and the intentionality behind inviting Ethan into the discussion. Ethan blinked in surprise, then straightened up, his eyes brightening as he realized he had the group's attention. He took a breath, and then his voice broke through the silence, offering insights and experiences that added depth to the conversation—perspectives that only someone in his position could provide.

The scene shifted once more. Mira found herself in the role of DeAnne, a volunteer coordinator at a local charity supporting immigrants and refugees. She was attending a planning meeting about new community programs. Mira could feel the dynamics at play—many of the volunteers, herself included, were making decisions without consulting the very people these programs would impact. Mira felt an uneasiness settling in, recognizing the imbalance of power. She spoke up, suggesting they form an advisory group made up of community members who were immigrants themselves so their voices could directly shape the services being offered. The other volunteers nodded thoughtfully, and Mira felt a sense of relief. It was about more than just creating programs—it was about ensuring that those affected had the power to shape their own experiences.

The scene dissolved, and Mira found herself back in the sanctuary, standing before Elara. The mirror had gone still, its glow soft and inviting. Mira felt tears prick at her eyes—she understood now the power of making space, of using her own position to invite others in.

"It's not about giving away power," Mira said, her voice full of emotion. "It's about sharing it. It's about making sure that everyone has the room they need to contribute."

Elara nodded, a quiet kindness shining in her eyes. "Exactly, Mira. But there's something important to remember: sharing power doesn't mean placing an unfair burden on marginalized people. We must be careful not to **tokenize** or rely on traditionally marginalized individuals to represent their entire demographic or solve inequities alone."

Mira frowned, reflecting on her recent experiences. "Oof. I've made that mistake before," she admitted. "Once, at work, I asked a Black woman to lead our Diversity, Equity, and Inclusion (DEI) committee without considering the time and burden it would place on her. It was right after George Floyd's murder by a policeman in Minneapolis, Minnesota, in 2020. I felt pressured to start a committee, but I hadn't taken the time to think through why I was doing it or what the committee was meant to achieve. I didn't stop to think about how unfair it was to expect her to take on that work simply because of her identity."

"That's part of the learning process," Elara said. "It's not about perfection, but progress. Sharing power means listening deeply, supporting others in ways that lighten their load, and ensuring equity by doing your part to address systemic issues."

Mira nodded slowly, the words sinking in. "So it's about collaboration—about making space, but also about doing the work myself to create that space?"

Elara smiled. "Exactly. **Allyship** is about understanding the spaces we occupy and recognizing when to step aside so that others can step forward. It's about lifting others and amplifying otherwise silenced or ignored voices."

Mira took a deep breath, her heart full. "How do I make sure I do this—not just today, but every day?"

Elara smiled, reaching for a piece of parchment. "This is your assignment, Mira. Reflect on the spaces you occupy—in meetings, in conversations, in your community. Ask yourself: Who isn't being heard? How can you create an opening for them? And most importantly, how can you make power-sharing an ongoing practice?"

Mira took the parchment, nodding slowly. "It's about being aware—about seeing where my privilege creates space for me and using that privilege to make space for others."

Elara's smile widened. "Indeed. Remember, Mira, power isn't diminished by sharing it—it grows. When we create space for others, we enrich the whole."

Mira left the sanctuary, realizing this next practice would be challenging—it meant constantly checking herself and making choices about when to step forward and when to step back. But she also knew it was crucial. Sharing power wasn't just about making others feel included; it was about building something bigger than herself—something that benefited everyone.

As she walked away from the sanctuary, she glanced at the parchment in her hand. Written at the bottom were words that would guide her practice: *Create space. Share power. Pass the mic.*

She smiled, a tentative confidence growing within her. She knew this work wouldn't always feel easy, but she was determined to try, step by imperfect step. It was time to share her power.

CHAPTER 20

Share Power
MIRA'S REFLECTION

Mira walked to her car after work one evening, the parchment from Elara still tucked into her bag. The words echoed in her mind: *Create space. Share power. Pass the mic.* She thought about what those words truly meant—not just in theory but in the everyday moments when she had the choice to share, step aside, or lift someone else up. Anxious to talk things through, Mira texted Ruby to invite her over.

That evening, they sat on the concrete deck by the lake, a sturdy bench built into the shore providing a comfortable spot to unwind. The water lapped gently against the edge, reflecting the soft glow of the moonlight. Fireflies flitted through the dense ground cover on the far side of the lake, their soft glow punctuating the darkness. The rhythmic croaks of frogs created a natural symphony, while the persistent buzz of mosquitoes filled the humid air. Mayflies emerged from the lake, their delicate forms drawn toward the warm glow of the house lights. Molly tore around the yard in hyperspeed circles, pausing only long enough to drop a slobbery ball at Mira's feet, her wagging tail daring anyone to resist another round of fetch. After some small talk and shared admiration of the beautiful night, Mira fidgeted with her glass, struggling to find the right words. Finally, she looked up, her voice hesitant but sincere.

"Ruby, I... I've been thinking a lot about us, about how I've been as a friend," Mira began, her eyes dropping to her hands. "I'm realizing how much I've missed. You've been so supportive of me, and I haven't always reciprocated the way I should have. I'm sorry for not being more aware." Tears welled in her eyes, and she blinked them back. "Especially... with how race plays a part."

Ruby tilted her head, her expression softening. "Mira, I've never felt like you weren't there for me. But I can tell this is something you're working through. What brought this on?"

Mira exhaled, her grip tightening on her glass. "It's this journey with Elara. She's opened my eyes to so much—about power, privilege, and how we hold space for others. And, Ruby, I've been realizing... I've been wearing blinders, only seeing what I wanted to see. Things you might have needed me to see. Like when we talked about that work meeting last year, or any of the many events at work that make you feel devalued, excluded, and discouraged. I—I brushed it all off, and I'm sorry."

Ruby's eyes softened further, and she reached across the bench, placing a hand over Mira's. "Thank you for saying that," she said gently. "It's hard to notice privilege, especially when it's invisible to you. I appreciate that you're reflecting on it now. But, Mira, I never doubted you cared. You're showing it even more now."

Mira's voice trembled. "I don't want to just try, Ruby. I want to do better. I'm learning how to step back, to ask what people need instead of assuming I know best. And I want to do that with you, too. So, please, tell me if there's ever a time when I'm not showing up the way you need. Or... if I'm letting my own discomfort get in the way. Like now, with these tears." She gave a nervous laugh, wiping at her cheeks. "I know I need to learn to sit with the hard stuff."

Ruby smiled, warmth radiating from her expression. "Mira, that means a lot. Honestly, just knowing you're this thoughtful about our friendship makes me feel valued. But if I ever need something different or feel like you aren't getting it, I'll let you know. And the same goes for you. Friendship is a two-way street, right?"

They both laughed softly, the tension easing.

"Ruby, can you help me think through something else on my mind?" Mira inquires.

"Sure, what's going on?" Ruby asked.

Mira hesitated for a moment, then began explaining, "It's about the boys that come around looking for a spot to fish on the lake. I... I told them they couldn't fish in my backyard anymore. My neighbors kept warning me that it's a private lake and brought up all these liability fears. It got to me, and I ended up saying no to them. At the time, it felt like I was protecting myself, but now it just feels wrong."

She paused, standing up and walking to the edge of the deck where she launches her kayak. Picking up a small pebble, she turned it over in her hand thoughtfully. With a quick flick of her wrist, she skipped it across the water, watching as it hopped once, twice, then disappeared with a soft plop. The ripples spread outward, mirroring her swirling thoughts. She sighed and turned back to Ruby. "At first, it felt like the right thing to do, but now I'm not so sure. I worked so hard to buy my first home, Ruby, and I value my privacy. I don't want people coming and going all the time. But then I think about those boys—they're just kids. I don't want to create another barrier for them either." Mira sighed. "And it feels so complicated. I don't think putting up a welcome sign is the answer, but I don't know what is."

Ruby listened intently, nodding as Mira spoke. "That's a tough one. You're right—it's your space, and you shouldn't feel forced to give it up completely. But maybe it doesn't have to be all or nothing. Maybe it's a conversation. You don't have to have all the answers right away, Mira. I think you're wrestling with something a lot of people don't even notice," Ruby said thoughtfully. "You have the power to say yes or no, and that's a privilege. But maybe it's not about a permanent yes or no. Maybe it's about finding a way to create something sustainable and fair."

As they packed things up to head back inside, Mira felt lighter. Her mind buzzed with ideas, and Ruby's encouragement and friendship steadied her heart. Their conversation had meandered through heavier reflections and lighter topics, but it left Mira with a renewed sense of commitment to her relationships. She knew the path wouldn't always be smooth—there would likely be stumbles, moments of discomfort, and even times when she unintentionally hurt others or herself. But she also recognized that the effort was worth it. Growth, she realized, wasn't about perfection; it was about persistence, vulnerability, and the willingness to try again, even after falling short. She realized that sharing power wasn't just about actions—it was about being vulnerable and intentional, especially as a friend.

The next morning at the office, Mira thought about how to put Elara's last lesson into practice. As she reflected on the words from Elara—*Create space. Share power. Pass the mic.*—she thought back to her conversation with Ruby and the little fishermen. These lessons weren't isolated; they intertwined in her efforts to balance boundaries, fairness, and her growing understanding of power dynamics. During the project planning meeting, an opportunity arose. The team was finalizing speakers for an upcoming presentation, and her boss looked to Mira, expecting her to take the lead as usual. Mira straightened, preparing to step forward as she always did. The spotlight was hers to claim, and for a moment, she hesitated. The familiar comfort of taking charge was hard to resist. In her mind, she wrestled with the thought: *Why shouldn't I take this? I've earned this role.*

But another voice reminded her of Elara's lesson: *Create space. Share power. Pass the mic.* She glanced at Camille, one of her colleagues. Camille had a quieter presence, but her expertise was undeniable. Still, Mira's first instinct pushed back: *What if she's not ready? What if it reflects poorly on the team?* Even as the thoughts swirled, she knew they stemmed from her own reluctance to let go.

Taking a deep breath, Mira finally spoke. "Actually," she began, her voice steady despite the internal conflict, "Camille should take the lead on this presentation. She's done incredible work on the details, and I know her insights will bring significant value."

Camille's eyes widened briefly, surprise evident. The boss paused, looked between them, and then tipped his head in agreement. "Great idea, Mira. Camille, are you ready for it?"

Camille took a moment to gather herself before responding with a confident smile. "Yes, absolutely. I'd love to." Mira felt a quiet satisfaction wash over her—this was what sharing power looked like in practice. It was a small shift, but it mattered.

Later that week, Mira attended a community meeting to support a neighborhood initiative. As she sat at the table, she realized something important: most decisions were being made by people like her—educated professionals who weren't directly affected by the issues being discussed. Mira spoke up, her voice amiable but firm.

"I think we're missing an important perspective here," she said, looking around the room. "We need to hear directly from the people impacted by these decisions. What if we formed an advisory group of community members—parents, students, residents—who can guide us on what they need?"

The room went quiet momentarily, and Mira could feel the shift—some people were uncomfortable, but others were nodding, considering her words. One of the organizers leaned forward, smiling. "That's a great idea, Mira. Let's make it happen."

Feeling encouraged, Mira took the next step without consulting anyone further. At the following meeting, she announced, "I've spoken with a few people and think it would be great if Sheila took the lead on organizing the advisory group." She glanced at Sheila, expecting a smile or nod, but instead saw hesitation flicker across her face.

Later, Sheila approached Mira privately. "I appreciate you thinking of me, but I'm not sure this is the right role for me right now. I wish you had asked me first." Mira's face flushed as the realization hit her—she had assumed Sheila's willingness without considering her voice in the process.

Mira apologized quickly. "You're absolutely right. I should have spoken with you first. I got so caught up in trying to share the responsibility that I forgot to collaborate. I'm sorry."

Sheila smiled, her tone forgiving. "It's okay. I know your intentions were good. But let's talk next time, alright?"

The exchange left Mira thoughtful. It was a small misstep, but it showed her that sharing power wasn't just about giving opportunities—it was about ensuring those opportunities aligned with the person's readiness and desires. It was a lesson she wouldn't forget.

As the week went on, Mira reflected on her actions and intentions. She realized that sharing power required constant effort. It was easy to slip into old habits and take the lead out of comfort, but she knew she was making a difference every time she paused and chose to make space.

As Mira sat with her thoughts, she wrote more in her journal:

Today, I shared the presentation with Camille. It felt right but also a little scary—letting go of that spotlight and trusting someone else to take it. But I saw her shine, and it reminded me that leader-

ship isn't about being the loudest voice in the room—it's about lifting others so everyone's voice is heard.

At the community meeting, I realized how easy it is to forget what it's like not to have a seat at the table. Sharing power means inviting others in and sometimes giving up my seat entirely. It's uncomfortable, but discomfort is part of growth. Sharing power isn't about diminishing my voice but allowing others to step into theirs. I remember the first time I felt truly heard in my engineering classes—it was transformative. If I can create that kind of space for others, maybe it could also make a difference in their journey.

I recognize that sometimes I might get it wrong. There may be times when I think I'm making space, but it could come across as taking over or assuming what's best. That's why accountability is key—I need to stay open to feedback and be willing to adjust if needed.

She took a deep breath, her pen moving across the page again:

Sharing power means seeing beyond my comfort. It means understanding when my privilege allows me to speak up and when it's time to step back and pass the proverbial mic.

Mira thought about the small ways she could make space in her everyday life—like choosing not to fill every silence in a meeting, waiting to see if others wanted to contribute, or inviting those who had been quiet to share their thoughts. It wasn't about grand actions but about cultivating awareness and a commitment to listening.

She looked out the window, the darkening sky spreading beyond her. She knew that sharing power was not about one-time actions but about changing her mindset—a shift in how she saw herself and her influence in every interaction. She wrote down her final thought for the evening:

Leadership is about creating space—recognizing my power and privilege and using it to uplift others. My success doesn't have to come at someone else's expense. Sometimes, it might feel like a personal sacrifice, but true growth and leadership come from helping others rise.

Mira set her pen down, feeling a mixture of exhaustion and fulfillment. The work wasn't easy, but it was important. It was about building something more significant than herself—creating a world where everyone could be heard and where everyone had a chance to contribute.

She picked up the parchment from Elara, the words written there guiding her thoughts:

Create space. Share power. Pass the mic.

These weren't just words anymore. They were becoming her way of being.

Mira closed her journal and leaned back in her chair, a quiet tenacity filling her. She was ready to keep going—to continue practicing, learning, and growing. She wanted to share her power, not just for herself but for everyone who needed it.

CHAPTER 21

Disrupt Barriers
ELARA'S LESSON

Mira entered Elara's sanctuary for the final lesson, her heart full of anticipation. She had explored her identity, biases, and how her power could lift others. Today, however, a deeper challenge lay ahead: confronting the institutional and systemic structures that uphold inequity.

Elara stood beside the mirror, her expression calm but serious. Mira sensed that today was different. The space's energy was heavier and charged with significance. The mirror shimmered softly, its light subdued, as if acknowledging the gravity of what was about to unfold.

"Mira," Elara began, her voice soothing yet firm. "You have come a long way. You have learned about your personhood, how to perceive others empathetically, and the power you hold. Today, we talk about the responsibility that comes with that power and the importance of understanding the larger systems at play."

Mira nodded, her eyes locked on Elara's. She sensed this lesson was not just about her—it was about everyone who may not have the same access, privilege, or power. She had felt the shift in her understanding during the last practice—the realization that sharing power meant actively making room for others. But she also knew deeper forces were at play—systems needing more than personal change.

"True inclusivity," Elara continued, "is not just about what happens between individuals. It's about the systems we live in—the rules, the norms, the practices that determine who has access, who is valued, and who is left out. These are systems rooted in power—ideologies established long ago to benefit specific groups. Today, you will explore these layers in a deeper way."

Elara paused momentarily, and her hand hovered briefly over the mirror, leading it to shimmer with latent power. "To create real change, we must understand the levels at which inequality is constructed and sustained. One way to approach this is by using the **Interlocking 4-I Model**.[4] This model helps us see how four interconnected levels of privilege and oppression work together: ideological, interpersonal, institutional, and internalized.

"At the ideological level, these are the core beliefs, biases, and stereotypes that have been ingrained in society. For example, beliefs that certain racial groups are inherently superior to others or that men are more capable leaders than women. Whether consciously or not, these ideas are often used to justify inequalities, such as restricting access to education or leadership roles, and form the foundation of systemic oppression.

"Next, the interpersonal level represents how these beliefs influence our interactions with one another. For example, a manager might unconsciously favor a male employee over a female one because of stereotypes about leadership abilities, or a teacher might expect less from students of a certain racial background. Stereotypes and biases influence how people treat each other, creating a social environment that either privileges or oppresses individuals based on their identity.

"The third level is institutional, where these ideologies are embedded into policies, practices, and cultural norms within institutions like schools, workplaces, and governments. For example, hiring practices that favor candidates from elite universities, zero-tolerance policies in schools that disproportionately affect marginalized students, or healthcare policies that fail to provide adequate services to certain communities. These structures often uphold and perpetuate inequalities through their policies and operations.

"Finally, the internalized level is about how individuals come to accept these external messages about their own worth and capabilities. For example, a young woman might internalize the belief that she is not suited for a leadership role because of societal messages that men are more competent leaders. Similarly, a

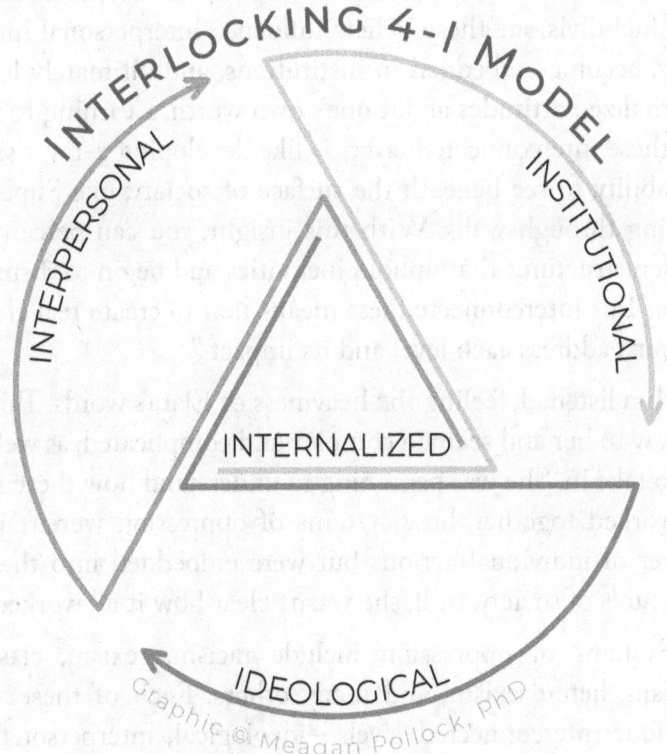

queer person might internalize heterosexism and homophobia, believing they are somehow less deserving of love or acceptance because of pervasive societal prejudice. When oppressed groups internalize beliefs that they are less deserving, they reenact the oppression on themselves. Privileged groups may internalize a sense of entitlement without fully realizing it. This self-reinforcing cycle ensures that systemic inequalities remain deeply embedded as people both consciously and unconsciously perpetuate these beliefs.

"These interconnected levels are at play in every community and institution, influencing societal structures and how we perceive ourselves and others."

Elara's voice took on a deeper resonance, emphasizing the importance of understanding the interconnected systems. "Ideological beliefs are the foundation, shaping stereotypes and biases that fuel division. These beliefs influence interpersonal interactions, become embedded in institutions, and ultimately lead to internalized attitudes about one's own worth. Learning to identify these interconnected layers is like developing x-ray vision—the ability to see beneath the surface of society, like Superman peering through walls. With this insight, you can perceive the hidden structures that uphold inequities and begin to dismantle them. This interconnectedness means that to create real change, we must address each level and its impact."

Mira listened, feeling the heaviness of Elara's words. This was all new to her and seemed complex and complicated, as well as a lot to take in. She was beginning to understand how these layers all worked together, how systems of oppression weren't just a matter of individual actions but were embedded into the very structures of society. Still, she wasn't clear how it all worked.

"Systems of oppression include racism, sexism, classism, ableism, heterosexism, and many others. Each of these -isms has four interconnected levels—ideological, interpersonal, institutional, and internalized—that reinforce one another. For instance, sexism is perpetuated through ideological beliefs that men are more competent, interpersonal behaviors that favor men over women, institutional policies that limit women's access to leadership positions, and internalized beliefs that make women doubt their own worth. When these systems overlap, they create compounding structures of inequity and inequality. This overlapping is known as intersectionality, a term coined by Kimberlé Crenshaw. **Intersectionality** helps us understand how different forms of oppression, such as racism, sexism, and classism, interconnect and create unique barriers for individuals who belong to multiple marginalized groups. For example, a Black woman might face both racism and sexism, which together create unique barriers that amplify the challenges she experiences. This overlapping of multiple systems of oppression can make it even harder for individuals to access opportunities or be treated fairly. They are embedded in our culture, institutions, and interactions—it's like they're in the very air we breathe," Elara continued. "These systems prioritize and privilege one group over another, and understanding them is crucial for change. With your power, Mira, comes the responsibility to challenge each level—ideological, interpersonal, institutional, and internalized—because only by addressing each can we dismantle these inequities."

Mira swallowed hard, her thoughts swirling with the weight of Elara's words. How could anyone possibly untangle so many deeply rooted systems? The complexity was staggering, and Mira felt a pang of self-doubt. She knew this was important, vital even, but it felt so far beyond her grasp.

"This is... a lot," she admitted, her voice quiet but steady. "I understand why this matters, but I don't even know where to start. How can one person make a difference against something so massive?"

Elara's expression softened, and she nodded, acknowledging Mira's overwhelm. "You're right, Mira. This is complex work, and it's not something you can solve alone. The first step is understanding—truly seeing the systems for what they are. That's where the mirror comes in. It will guide you, showing you how these layers play out in the lives of real people and the choices they face. Learning to see and act with intention is the foundation of this journey."

She gestured toward the mirror, which began to shimmer again. "Today, the mirror will give you a glimpse of what it means to confront and dismantle these systemic barriers. You will embody individuals who are actively using their power and influence to create change within their communities, workplaces, and schools. Addressing systemic oppression means challenging comfort zones, questioning longstanding norms, and working through discomfort for the greater good. The mirror will help you identify the Interlocking 4-I's. Are you ready?"

Mira hesitated, her fingers trembling slightly as she clasped her hands together. "I… I'm not sure I'm ready," she admitted her voice a mix of doubt and determination. She glanced at Elara, seeking reassurance. "But I'll try."

She closed her eyes as Elara spoke softly and felt the familiar warmth of the mirror surround her. When she opened her eyes, she found herself sitting at a large boardroom table, the nameplate in front of her reading "Anna Reyes, Director of People Operations." Mira felt the confidence of the position but also the challenge of what lay ahead. Around her, she saw the faces of the other directors—mostly men, mostly White. They were discussing a new set of hiring policies, and Mira could sense the unease in the room.

One of the men, a senior executive, spoke up. "I think we should keep things as they are. Our current policies have worked for years—why change something that's not broken?"

Mira felt Anna's heartbeat quicken, a mix of nerves and determination coursing through her. She knew this was a pivotal moment, and she had to speak out despite the discomfort it would create. She cleared her throat, feeling the weight of the room's gaze on her. "I disagree," she began, her voice temperate but assertive. "Our current policies may have worked for some, but they haven't worked for everyone. We need an environment where people from all backgrounds can thrive—not just those who have historically benefited."

She felt a ripple of discomfort around the table, but she pressed on. "I've reviewed our hiring data, and it's clear that we're not reaching people from underrepresented communities. We need to change our approach—to actively recruit from different networks, re-evaluate our job descriptions for biased language, train our interviewers, and create a process that supports candidates from diverse backgrounds. This isn't just about numbers. It's about creating an inclusive workplace that reflects the community's diversity."

The room was silent for a moment, the tension thick in the air. Mira could feel the resistance—the discomfort that came with challenging the status quo. She also heard whispers between colleagues, some expressing doubt and others annoyance. She overheard one whisper, "This could take jobs away from the people who've always been here." The underlying fear was palpable—fear of change, fear that adjusting the system could displace those who had historically benefited.

Anna took a steadying breath and continued, her voice calm but resolute. "I understand the concern about change, but let's remember why this matters. There is a strong business case for diversity. Studies consistently show that diverse teams are more innovative and perform better financially. If we want to remain competitive, we can't afford to overlook talent simply because it comes from different backgrounds."

She paused, allowing her words to settle. "Beyond that, aligning our hiring practices with our stated values is essential. We claim to value inclusion, yet our current practices don't reflect that. This is our chance to make sure our actions align with our principles. By making these changes, we're not just doing what's right—we're building a stronger company that truly lives up to its ideals."

Mira felt a newfound determination—an understanding that this was the right path, even if it was fraught with challenges. Slowly, she saw a few directors nodding, their expressions softening. Others still seemed reluctant, but Mira could see the beginning of a shift.

Elara's voice echoed in her mind: "With power comes responsibility. Creating true change means embracing discomfort and stepping into the unknown."

Mira recognized the Interlocking 4-I's at play in Anna's situation. Ideologically, the belief that the current system was 'fair' perpetuated the privilege of those already in power, rooted in classism and the underlying belief that the 'best' candidates were already being chosen. This ideology was influenced by racism and sexism, favoring White male employees as inherently more capable. Interpersonally, Anna could feel the tension between her and the senior executive, who dismissed the idea of change—this reflected biases in their interactions, where Anna's perspective as a woman of color was likely undervalued compared to her male colleagues. Institutionally, the company policies had clearly been designed to benefit those with traditional qualifications, favoring a predominantly White male pool of candidates, which upheld systemic barriers for underrepresented groups. Finally, at the internalized level, some employees from underrepresented backgrounds might have internalized the message that they were not as deserving of these roles, doubting their capabilities and feeling that they shouldn't apply.

The scene shifted, and Mira found herself in another setting—a school board meeting. She was now in the body of Mr. Patel, a community advocate. He was standing before the board, proposing to change the curriculum to include more diverse voices—to teach history that wasn't just centered on dominant narratives but included the stories of marginalized communities like Indigenous people groups, African Americans, LGBTQ+ individuals, and immigrants.

Mira could feel the pushback from some of the board members—the arguments about "tradition" and "standards." One board member even interrupted Mr. Patel, saying, "Parents might not be comfortable with this. It's too radical." But Mira also felt the support of the parents and students who had come to the meeting; their presence was a reminder of why this work mattered. She spoke with conviction, her voice unwavering. "All of our children deserve to see themselves in their education, too. They deserve to learn the truth about our history—all of it, not just the comfortable parts. This is how we create productive and engaged citizens who contribute positively to society, and ultimately a more just and equitable world."

The tension was undeniable, but so was the hope in the room. Mira could feel the parents' energy behind her; their silent encouragement gave her the strength to stand firm. She realized that systemic change wasn't about pleasing everyone but about doing what was right, even when it made others uncomfortable or afraid. Mira recalled hearing some of the White parents say, "I don't want my kids feeling bad about themselves," reflecting a common resistance to confronting the uncomfortable truths of history, such as the mass human trafficking and enslavement of Africans and the genocide of Indigenous peoples. She understood that this fear stemmed from a desire to protect their children from discomfort, but in doing so, it also prevented crucial growth and the opportunity to acknowledge and learn from historical injustices. Systemic change requires courage—to face discomfort, to learn, and to push through resistance to make a lasting impact.

In this scenario, Mira saw how the Interlocking 4-I's operated. Ideologically, the resistance to including diverse histories was rooted in the belief that only dominant narratives were valuable. This belief was underpinned by racism and **xenophobia**, favoring White, Eurocentric perspectives over others. Interpersonally, Mr. Patel felt the discomfort and pushback from some board members who resisted change, reflecting biases and prejudices in their interactions that subtly conveyed whose voices were prioritized. Institutionally, the curriculum policies were exclusionary, maintaining inequity by focusing solely on dominant voices, thereby systematically erasing the histories and contributions of marginalized groups. Internally, both students and educators from marginalized backgrounds may have internalized the idea that their histories and contributions were less important, making it harder for them to see their value in the educational context.

The mirror shimmered again, and Mira found herself in a new scenario—a corporate workshop led by a Human Resources professional named Carlos. Mira, embodying Carlos, was leading a discussion about equitable promotion practices within the company. One participant, a senior manager, rolled his eyes and said, "Why do we need to cater to everyone's needs? Shouldn't promotions be purely about merit?"

Mira felt Carlos's frustration. "The idea of **meritocracy** is flawed," she replied. "It assumes everyone starts from the same place, with the same opportunities, but that's not true. People face different barriers that hold them back—barriers like biases in hiring, limited access to education, and stereotypes that shape how they are treated. If we don't recognize these barriers, we keep things unfair, even if we don't mean to. True fairness means understanding these obstacles and doing what we can to level the playing field so everyone has a fair chance to succeed."

Mira recognized the Interlocking 4-I's at play in this scenario. Ideologically, the belief in a pure meritocracy perpetuated the idea that everyone had the same opportunities, ignoring systemic inequalities—a belief often rooted in classism and racism, as it presumes all candidates have equal access to resources and networks. Interpersonally, the senior manager's dismissive reaction illustrated how interpersonal biases affect attitudes toward systemic change, displaying a lack of empathy and understanding for marginalized employees. Institutionally, the company's promotion policies did not take systemic disadvantages into account, such as the unequal access to opportunities faced by marginalized groups, thereby reinforcing inequity. Internally, employees from underrepresented backgrounds may have internalized these systemic messages, feeling inherently less deserving of advancement. The myth of meritocracy can often lead to self-doubt and discourage them from aspiring to leadership roles, further perpetuating inequities in the workplace.

The mirror shimmered yet again, and Mira found herself in a new scenario—this time at a community meeting held in a local neighborhood center. Mira embodied Ms. Johnson, a community leader advocating for fair housing, support for small businesses, and addressing **food desert** and **food mirage** issues in her neighborhood. The room was filled with local residents, some anxious, some hopeful. They were gathered to discuss revitalizing their community—one that had long been neglected by policymakers and developers.

Ms. Johnson stood up, her voice steady, and began, "Our community deserves the same opportunities as any other. We are facing overlapping challenges—lack of affordable housing, limited access to affordable healthy food, and small businesses struggling to survive. We need solutions that address all these needs together."

Mira, as Ms. Johnson, recognized the Interlocking 4-I's at play. Ideologically, the belief that poorer neighborhoods did not warrant investment was rooted in classism and often racism, as historically marginalized communities were left out of the conversation about development. Interpersonally, Mira could see how residents often felt disregarded by local officials, who showed up infrequently and with condescending attitudes, reflecting the biases that shaped their interactions. Institutionally, city policies had prioritized wealthy developers and ignored the needs of low-income residents, resulting in a lack of grocery stores, affordable housing, and economic opportunities. Internally, many community members had internalized the belief that they were not deserving of better conditions, accepting neglect as the norm and feeling powerless to demand change.

Ms. Johnson continued, "We need access to affordable housing that allows families to stay here. We need incentives for grocery stores to come into our neighborhood so our children can grow up healthy. We need to support our local businesses—the heart of our community. I propose petitioning the city council for a dedicated community development fund that focuses on these issues together. We need your voices—every single one of you—to make this happen."

Mira could feel the energy shift in the room—people sitting up straighter, nodding in agreement. She knew that addressing these systemic issues would require challenging entrenched beliefs and pushing local institutions to see the value in their community. The officials' discomfort and the residents' hesitation to believe in change were all barriers that could be overcome with collective action and perseverance. Slowly, hands began to raise, and people were willing to join the fight for a better future. The momentum was beginning, and Mira knew this was just the start of creating lasting change.

The mirror shimmered once more, and Mira found herself back in Elara's sanctuary, her heart pounding. She looked at Elara, her stance resolute with purpose. "Wow," she said, her voice thick with emotion. "It's not enough to just share power—I have to use my position to challenge the systems that keep people out. It's about creating real change, even when it's uncomfortable."

Elara nodded, her expression proud. "Yes, Mira. True inclusivity means going beyond individual actions to examine the systems around us. Ask yourself: Who benefits? Who is left out? And how can you change that? Use your power to create openings, break down barriers, and build something better for everyone."

She handed Mira a fresh piece of glowing parchment. "Your assignment is to take what you've learned and apply it. Look at the systems you're a part of—at work, in your community, and even in your personal life. Identify the barriers, see who is being left out, and use your power to make a difference."

Mira took the parchment, which sparkled as she made contact with it, her hands steady. She felt the weight of responsibility but also the clarity of purpose. "With power comes responsibility," she whispered, echoing Elara's earlier words.

Elara smiled, her eyes shining. "Yes, Mira. And you have the power to make a difference. Use it wisely."

Mira left the sanctuary that day with a sense of resolve. This was her final practice, but it was only the beginning of her work. She knew that challenging systemic barriers wouldn't be easy—it would be uncomfortable, require courage and collaboration, and take time. But she also knew that it was necessary. True change would not happen by staying comfortable—it required pushing boundaries, challenging the status quo, and building what could be.

As she walked away, she looked at the parchment in her hand. Written at the bottom were the words: *Challenge the system. Create change. Use your power for good.*

Mira smiled, a steady resolve taking root within her. It was time to take action.

CHAPTER 22

Disrupt Barriers

MIRA'S REFLECTION

It had been months since Mira last stepped into Elara's sanctuary. The lessons she had learned from the mirror still resonated within her, echoing in her thoughts every day. Challenging systemic barriers wasn't an easy task—it was the hardest one she'd faced. There was no immediate transformation, no instant success. This work was different. It required patience, persistence, and a willingness to meet resistance head-on.

Mira sat at her kitchen table, her journal open in front of her. The early morning sun filtered through the curtains, bathing the room in a soft, hopeful light. She ran her fingers over the pages, tracing the notes she had scribbled throughout the past few months—notes about her attempts to challenge the systems she was part of.

There had been moments of progress. Mira remembered the board meeting where she had raised questions about the promotion criteria within her department, pointing out how those criteria inadvertently kept out people from marginalized backgrounds. She had mapped out the Interlocking 4-I's at play: ideologically, the belief in a 'fair' system that ignored existing privileges; interpersonally, the dismissive reactions from colleagues reflecting biases; institutionally, the policies that favored certain educational backgrounds and experiences; and internally, the self-doubt among those from underrepresented groups who felt they weren't deserving. This mapping helped her articulate the need for change more clearly. It wasn't an easy conversation; there were skeptical glances, pushback, and comments about meritocracy. But Mira had held her ground, patiently explaining that equity wasn't about lowering standards—it was about understanding that not everyone starts from the same place and that true fairness meant leveling the playing field.

The weeks following that meeting had been challenging. She had to confront not only the discomfort of her colleagues but also her own—the doubts, the fears of overstepping, and the fear of failure. But she reminded herself that discomfort was part of the journey. She leaned on the lessons from Elara—that with power came responsibility, and real change was often uncomfortable.

Mira turned the page in her journal, her eyes catching on a note she had written months ago: *Challenge the system. Create change. Use your power for good.* She smiled, remembering Elara's voice as she had handed her that final piece of parchment. The words had become a sort of mantra for her, a guiding principle as she navigated the complexities of her work and her role within her community.

She thought about the community project she had become involved with—an initiative to create more inclusive public spaces in her city. Mira used the Interlocking 4-I's framework to identify barriers excluding certain groups. Ideologically, there was a long-standing belief that certain neighborhoods didn't need investment; interpersonally, local leaders often dismissed the needs of marginalized residents; institutionally, the zoning laws and budget allocations perpetuated these inequities; and internally, many community members had accepted that their neighborhoods were less deserving. By systematically breaking down these barriers, Mira could advocate effectively for change. Mira had joined the committee initially just to lend a helping hand, but soon, she stepped into a leadership role. She used her voice to make sure that the voices of those often left out—people with disabilities, immigrants, young people—were not only included but amplified. She realized that creating equitable change meant not just making decisions for others but involving them in the decision-making process.

One of the biggest takeaways from her time away from Elara was understanding the difference between helping and empowering. In her previous efforts, she often thought of herself as someone who needed to help—to offer her resources, her voice, her influence. But what she had come to realize was that true power-sharing wasn't about stepping in to help—it was about stepping back to create space for others to take the lead, to use their own voices. It was about empowering others to have agency and to shape the systems that affected their lives. And sometimes, it meant Mira had to step out of the spotlight entirely, to pass the mic, or to give up her seat at the table.

Mira picked up her pen and began to write in her journal:

My positionality gives me power, but it also creates gaps in my perspective. Some days, it feels like those gaps are insurmountable, like no matter how much I try to listen or learn, I'm always a step behind. Challenging systemic barriers requires humility—and that's harder than I ever imagined. I don't have all the answers, and sometimes, I'm not even sure I'm asking the right questions. It's frustrating, humbling, and exhausting to confront the limits of my understanding. But I'm learning that it's not about being the hero. It's about sitting in that discomfort and still doing the work—creating a world where we all have the chance to thrive. That means not just opening doors for others to succeed but stepping aside so others can lead.

Mira paused, looking out the window at the world outside. She saw her neighbor walking his dog, a mother rushing her children into the car, and a young couple jogging together. The world was full of different stories and experiences. She grabbed her coffee and walked to the backyard, where Molly was playing with the neighborhood boys. Their laughter echoed as they cast their lines off the dock, joyfully fishing together. Mira smiled, feeling the warmth of connection, and she knew now that her role wasn't just to be aware of her own story, her own power—it was to use her understanding to break down the barriers that kept others from being heard, from having their contributions valued, and from accessing the opportunities they deserve.

She remembered one particular moment from the past month—an interaction with a young colleague named Brittany. Mira had encouraged Brittany to think through the systemic layers impacting her experiences. They discussed the ideological beliefs about who is heard in the workplace, the interpersonal dynamics that silenced her contributions, the institutional norms that shaped meeting conduct, and the internalized self-doubt Brittany had carried. By understanding these layers, Brittany felt empowered to take a different approach. Brittany had shared with Mira her frustrations about feeling overlooked in meetings and how her ideas were often ignored until someone else—usually a man—repeated them. Mira had felt a pang of recognition, remembering her experiences earlier in her career. Instead of offering advice or trying to fix things for Brittany, Mira had asked her how she wanted to address it. Together, they strategized a plan—not one where Mira would step in to rescue, but one where Brittany could take the lead, with Mira as her ally and advocate. It was a small step, but it was powerful. And when Brittany's voice was finally heard, Mira felt a deep sense of fulfillment—not because she had helped, but because she had created the space for Brittany to help herself.

Mira reflected on the three core themes of her journey—Personhood, Perception, and Power—and how they had become interwoven in her life. As she deepened her understanding of the Interlocking 4-I's of oppression, she realized how these themes were constantly influencing and shaping her actions. **Personhood** had given her the foundation to understand who she was, beyond labels, and to embrace every aspect of her identity. Through **Perception**, she learned to see others more clearly, recognize her biases, and understand that everyone moves through life with different filters shaped by their experiences. **Power** had taught her how to not only wield her influence with intention but also to share it meaningfully, to lift others up, and to work toward dismantling the systemic barriers—ideological, interpersonal, institutional, and internalized—that held people back.

Her journey with Elara had shown her that Personhood, Perception, and Power were deeply interconnected. It was a cycle of continuous growth, with each step reinforcing the lessons she had learned and broadening her understanding of herself and the world around her.

Mira closed her journal, a sense of peace washing over her. She knew she had more to learn, more to do. The journey wasn't over. She still faced resistance, she still made mistakes, and she still had moments where her own biases and fears got in the way. But she also knew that she was committed to the work—committed to challenging the systems around her, to using her power with intention, and to lifting others up, not by speaking for them, but by making sure they had the opportunity to speak for themselves.

She glanced at the calendar on her wall, noting the date she had circled—her next visit to Elara. It had been a long time, but she was ready to return, to share what she had learned, and to continue her journey. Because if there was one thing she knew for certain, it was that this work never truly ended. And that was what made it so meaningful.

Mira stood, her heart lighter, her purpose clearer. She was ready to keep going—to challenge, to learn, to grow, and to create change, one step at a time.

Moving Forward

CHAPTER 23

Reflect on the Journey

Mira walked slowly towards Elara's secluded sanctuary, a gentle breeze brushing against her face as she took in the familiar sights. It felt strange, yet comforting, to be returning after all these months. This time, she wasn't coming with questions, fears, or uncertainties. She was coming to close a chapter, to share what she had learned, and to understand what lay ahead.

Mira approached, Elara greeted her with a warm smile, her eyes glinting with a deep and quiet wisdom. With a fluid motion, Elara waved her hand over the seat by the mirror, and a faint shimmer danced around it, inviting Mira to sit. Mira settled in, the seat exuding a subtle warmth that made her feel both reposed and prepared.

"Welcome back, Mira," Elara said, her voice upbeat and encouraging. "It's good to see you. How have you been?"

Mira smiled, taking a deep breath. "It's been challenging," she said honestly. "But in the best way possible. My journey with you and the Magic Mirror to illuminate my **Positionality Prism** has reshaped how I understand myself and the world. I've grown by exploring the three P's—**Personhood, Perception**, and **Power**—delving into who I am, how I see others, and how I can use my influence to challenge barriers and share power. The nine practices I've embraced—like reflecting on my identity, checking my filter, and disrupting barriers—have guided me every step of the way. I came back today because I want to reflect on it all—the entire journey—and bring it together."

Elara nodded, her eyes soft. "Yes, let's do that. Let's start where you began. Do you remember what brought you here in the first place?"

Mira took a moment, thinking back to that morning in the coffee shop—the overwhelming feeling of not knowing how to help her friend Ruby, the desire to be a better leader, a better person. "I came here because I wanted to understand how I could make a meaningful difference," she said quietly. "I didn't know where to begin, but I knew something had to change. I wanted to be better for myself and for the people around me."

Elara smiled. "And you did. You've come a long way, Mira. You've explored Personhood, Perception, and Power. Each of these areas was key to unlocking the impact you wanted to have. Let's recap what you've learned."

Mira nodded, her heart warming. "**Personhood** was the first part of the journey," she said, her voice steady. "It was about understanding who I am—recognizing the different layers of my identity, the privileges I hold, and the challenges I face. I learned that understanding myself—my background, my beliefs, my identities—was essential. It was the foundation for everything else. It allowed me to see how my experiences shape my worldview, and how my positionality influences how I interact with others."

Elara nodded, adding, "You learned three practices during this part of the journey—**Explore Your Identity**, **Assess Salient Roles**, and **Identify Bridges and Barriers**. Each practice was a step deeper into self-awareness, helping you understand how you fit into the broader social landscape."

Mira smiled, recalling the challenging moments of self-reflection. "It was uncomfortable at times," she admitted. "But it was so important. Then came the theme of **Perception**—how I see others and how others see me. I learned that perception is like a filter—we filter everything and everyone through our own experiences unless we take intentional action to see things differently. That's what empathy-driven perspective-taking was about. It was about stepping out of my own lens and trying to see the world through someone else's eyes."

"Yes," Elara said. "You practiced **Check Your Filter, Expand Your Perspective**, and **See Beyond Yourself**. Each of these practices allowed you to better understand the perspectives of those around you, to challenge your own biases, and to build meaningful connections."

Mira nodded, a thoughtful expression crossing her face. "It was eye-opening," she said softly. "I realized that sometimes people's reactions to me aren't about me at all—they're a response to their own lived experiences, to the ways they've been treated by others in the past. It's about understanding that perception might not be reality, but it's someone's reality as a means of protecting themselves. I learned how to stay open, to respond with empathy rather than defensiveness."

Elara smiled, her eyes shining. "And finally, you learned about **Power**—how to use the power you have to create equitable change. Power is complex, but when we understand it, we can use it for good. You learned about the positionality practices: **Recognize Your Power, Share Power**, and **Disrupt Barriers**."

Mira's face brightened. "This part of the journey was the hardest, but it was also the most rewarding. I learned that having power means having responsibility—not just to help others but to create space for others to lead. I learned to share power, challenge the systems that uphold inequity, and step back when necessary so others can step forward. It's not about being the hero. It's about making sure everyone has the opportunity to thrive."

Elara nodded. "You've grown immensely, Mira. The journey of positionality—exploring personhood, perception, and power—isn't a one-time process. It's ongoing. It's about continually reflecting, questioning, and growing. But you've taken the steps to truly see yourself and others. You've embraced the discomfort, faced your fears, and used your power to create positive change. That's the real work of allyship and leadership."

Mira's eyes were misty, her heart full. "I couldn't have done this without you, Elara," she said, her voice thick with emotion. "You helped me see things I couldn't see on my own. You helped me become closer to the person I wanted to be—the kind of person who doesn't just mean well, but who does well."

Elara reached out, resting a hand on Mira's shoulder. "The magic was always within you, Mira. I just helped you find it. And now, it's up to you to continue the journey—to take what you've learned and use it to make a difference in the world. The mirror is always here for you, but you have the tools now. You know what to do."

Mira took a deep breath, a sense of resolve settling in her chest. "I do," she said firmly. "I know that the work is never over. I know I'll make mistakes, and I'll have to keep learning. But I'm ready. I'm ready to keep growing, to keep challenging, to keep making space for others."

Elara smiled, a look of pride in her eyes. "Then go, Mira. The world needs people like you—people who are willing to do the work, to create change, to make space for others. Keep examining life through your **Positionality Prism**, keep asking questions, keep challenging the status quo, and most importantly, keep your heart open."

Mira stood, feeling lighter, stronger, and more grounded than she ever had before. She looked at the mirror one last time, the shimmering surface reflecting her image back at her—an image of someone who was no longer afraid to face herself, to face the world, and to make a difference.

"Thank you, Elara," she whispered, her voice filled with gratitude. And with that, she turned and walked out of the sanctuary, ready to face whatever came next—one step at a time.

CHAPTER 24

Spread the Word

Mira stood before a group of people gathered in a community center. She had been invited to speak about her journey, but today was different. Today, she wasn't speaking as a student seeking wisdom. Today, she spoke as someone who had walked the path, learned the practices, and now wished to share her story with others, inviting them to take up the journey for themselves. She cleared her throat, her eyes moving across the crowd, finding both familiar and unfamiliar faces.

"When I began my journey, I thought I needed something extraordinary—something like a Magic Mirror to help me see the things I couldn't on my own. And for a while, that's exactly what I had," Mira started, her voice carrying through the quiet room. "But what I've come to realize is that the Magic Mirror is all around us if only we choose to look."

The room was silent; each face turned toward her, their attention unwavering. Mira paused for a moment, letting the weight of her words settle.

"You don't need a mirror to start this journey," she continued. "The tools, the lessons, the reflections—they're all available to each of us. The journey of understanding yourself, of seeing the world through different perspectives, of using your power for good—it's a journey anyone can take. It's not easy, and it's not quick, but it is worthwhile. And most importantly, you're not alone. In fact, it's a journey best done in community with others."

Mira smiled, remembering Elara's words and how she'd been told that the magic was always within her. She felt that now, a deep knowing that what she had learned could be shared, passed on, and made meaningful in the lives of others.

"The first step is understanding Personhood," Mira said, her eyes meeting those of a young woman in the front row. "It's about understanding who you are—your identities, your privileges, and your challenges. Ask yourself: Who am I, and how do my experiences shape the way I see the world? Use tools like the social identity map to explore your own layers and understand the facets that make you who you are. The goal isn't to have all the answers, but to start asking questions, to see yourself in a fuller, richer way."

Mira continued, "The next part of the journey is about Perception. We all see the world through a lens colored by our experiences. This lens—our positionality—acts as a filter, and sometimes, it shields us from the realities of others. So, practice empathy-driven perspective-taking. Before reacting, pause and ask yourself, 'What else might be true?'" Mira held up her hand, counting off her fingers. "Five fingers. Five possible truths. It's a simple gesture that has a profound impact. This practice can take you outside of your own filter and allow you to connect with others in meaningful ways."

She glanced at the audience, her eyes resting on a man who was nodding thoughtfully. "Perspective-taking helps us to understand how our biases might cloud our judgment. It also helps us understand that sometimes, how others perceive us is based on their past experiences—not necessarily on who we are. This means that sometimes we need to be the bridge, to extend understanding, and to stay open even when it's hard."

"And finally," Mira said, her voice growing stronger, "we must learn to understand Power—our own power, and how to use it ethically and effectively. Power isn't just about having authority; it's about recognizing your influence, sharing it, and creating opportunities for others. If you're in a position of power, ask yourself—how can I share this power? How can I make space for someone else who hasn't been given the same opportunities?"

Mira paused, her heart swelling as she remembered all that she had learned. "Throughout this journey, I've learned that with power comes responsibility. We have to be accountable—to ourselves, to those we lead, and to the systems we're a part of. It's not enough to mean well. We must do well. We must take action when we see harm. We must use our voices to amplify others and our privilege to break down barriers. And most importantly, we must be willing to keep learning, to keep reflecting, and to keep growing."

Mira looked out at the crowd, her gaze softening. "You don't need a Magic Mirror to do this work. The Magic Mirror is everywhere—in our conversations, in our reflections, in our willingness to be vulnerable and open. The journey isn't about perfection; it's about practice. It's about taking one step, then another, and another. And when you fall, it's about getting up, learning, and continuing the journey."

She smiled brilliantly with hope and assurance. "I'm inviting you to start this journey—to explore your personhood, to broaden your perception, and to use your power to create change. Think of it as looking through a prism—each facet offering a new perspective, a way to see the world differently and more clearly. One practice at a time, one step at a time. And when it gets hard—when you make mistakes, when you feel discouraged—remember that you're not alone. We're all on this journey together, and together, we can make a difference."

Mira took a deep breath, her eyes scanning the room. "So, here's your call to action: Start now. Take the first step. Reflect on who you are, challenge your biases, share your power, and always, always ask—'What else might be true?' The world needs you. We need each other. Let's do the work, let's be the change, and let's build a world where everyone has the opportunity to thrive."

The room was quiet, but Mira could see the spark in their eyes, the burgeoning curiosity and determination that she had felt on her own journey. She knew it wouldn't be easy for them, just as it hadn't been easy for her. But she also knew it would be worth it.

"The Magic Mirror," she said, her voice barely above a whisper, "is all around us. It's in each of us. Let's use it."

With that, she stepped back, her heart light, her purpose clear. The journey wasn't over. It never would be. And that was what made it beautiful.

Thank you for reading Magic Mirror. If this story resonated with you, please share its magic by telling your friends and colleagues or leaving a review. Your voice is the most powerful way to help others discover this journey. Thank you for your support!

CHAPTER 25

A Note From The Author

What is the *Magic Mirror*? It reflects what's there—your image, your surroundings—but also invites you to look deeper. It can be a tool for self-awareness, a portal to introspection, or a spark for transformation. The *Magic Mirror* is all these things: a reflection of who we are in the world and a call to see beyond what's immediately visible. It asks us to pause, to look, and to consider: Who are we? What do we see? How do we act?

When I began to understand the power of positionality, it felt like the world cracked open. As a woman in engineering, I often stood out—whether as the only woman in a class of 70 or the only woman on an engineering team. My age and gender compounded feelings of marginalization in a "pay your dues" industry culture, creating a tension I couldn't ignore. Later, as a researcher studying the experiences of young women in high school engineering, I realized how my perspective as both a woman and an engineer shaped my approach and how my lived experiences informed, but also limited, my understanding.

The first shift came during my doctoral studies when I encountered pivotal concepts that challenged my worldview. Reading about privilege through Dr. Peggy McIntosh's "Unpacking the Invisible Knapsack" offered my first real glimpse of its pervasive influence. A class on gender and science expanded my understanding of social constructs like race and gender. Choosing intersectionality (coined by legal scholar Kimberlé Crenshaw) as the framework for my dissertation brought clarity to my work while also revealing the gaps in my understanding.

Years of study had yet to fully reveal the systemic nature of oppression. Even though professors and colleagues urged me to explore systemic perspectives, I just couldn't see it. It felt like trying to see an image in a MagicEye puzzle that refused to come into focus for me, even as everyone around me seemed to see it effortlessly. Finally, a simple but powerful explanation of the four I's of oppression—ideological, interpersonal, institutional, and internalized—as seen through a Lego stop-motion video finally brought the pieces together and the hidden systems into focus. This moment was humbling, filled with both a reckoning of my past unawareness and the realization that I could now understand how systems functioned, transforming how I approached my work and illuminating the systemic barriers that had previously been invisible to me. With intentional study and exploration, why did it take me so long to see and understand the systems? Because of my positionality. It was a turning point.

POSITIONALITY STATEMENTS: In research and writing, positionality statements are increasingly common to situate authors in their work. Journals like the Journal of Women and Minorities in Science and Engineering now require them, recognizing their importance as reflexive practices. Such statements help clarify how identities shape decisions and foster humility, transparency, and justice.

So, what is my positionality?

I am a single, White, educated, middle-class, middle-aged, queer-identifying woman, business owner, and humanist who has multiple hidden disabilities.

A middle child between two brothers, my white evangelical parents raised us in a deeply conservative Southern Baptist, middle-income Texas household. After over two decades away, in 2022, I relocated back to the small Republican-stronghold town that grew me, Orange, Texas, to be closer to my parents. I am a licensed foster parent and hope to adopt someday.

I am a product of public schools. Academic scholarships and fellowships funded all three of my degrees (BS in Computer Science, MS in Electrical Engineering, PhD in Engineering Education). My education has been a class equalizer for me in many ways.

As a woman in computer science and engineering, I know what it feels like to be the only woman in the classroom, lab, fab, or conference room. My experiences working at Texas Instruments drove me to focus my career on changing the culture and climate of engineering and tech so that people from marginalized or minoritized backgrounds feel valued, included, encouraged, and affirmed in the classroom and workplace. My work has since expanded to multiple industries and fields.

Because I have lived it and continue to navigate a community and state where these ideas are frequently met with opposition, I understand the resistance and confusion that often come with confronting privilege. This lived experience enables me to guide others with empathy and strategy, helping them advance on their journey and learning practices to become better leaders, educators, colleagues, neighbors, friends, and more. My journey has forged my mission: to help others move from awareness to action faster.

Author's Note

Scaffolding Understanding

With tools and guidance, recognizing and addressing systemic barriers can be significantly accelerated for others. The **Positionality Prism**, the backbone framework of this book, emerged from a series of tools and services I developed to help others better understand their identities, privileges, and roles within larger systems—a vital step toward creating meaningful change. What I've learned from my journey to understand positionality and systems and a decade of experience teaching it to others is that discussing identity—race, gender, class, and more—can feel as unfamiliar as algebra might to someone encountering variables for the first time. During an algebra lesson, my former foster daughter Jaz once asked, "Why do we have to have letters mixed in with the numbers now?" Similarly, those unaccustomed to reflecting on identity often ask, "Why do we need to talk about this?" Although my heart longs to begin with the critical topic of systems of oppression, I recognize that diving directly into such subjects can alienate those new to the conversation or historically averse to it. Instead, I carefully structured the book's content and vocabulary to build understanding incrementally, one step at a time. By taking this approach, this book introduces readers to complex concepts through a scaffolded design grounded in learning theory, ensuring accessibility and clarity. My hope is that this book meets readers where they are and provides the care, clarity, and guidance needed to do this vital work.

Magic Mirror is a tool for reflection, discovery, and bold action—a resource I wish I could have shared with my younger self to shorten the years of wandering and hesitation. The name Mira, from the Spanish word for "look," reminds us to pause and truly see ourselves and the systems around us. Likewise, Elara, derived from the Spanish word "luz," meaning "light," symbolizes the positivity and guiding force we can become when we embrace this work. Through its guidance, I hope this book will illuminate your path and help you on your journey to see yourself, others, and the world differently.

I invite you to connect with me if I can support you in your journey to **Intentionally Engineer Inclusion®**. Together, we can create meaningful change through thoughtful reflection, deliberate action, and the practical application of the nine practices outlined in this book.

With gratitude,

Meagan Pollock, PhD

Your Journey Doesn't End Here

Thank you for exploring the ideas and strategies in this book. The learning doesn't stop here—this is just the beginning!

Visit **MagicMirrorBook.com** for access to a wide range of additional tools and opportunities designed to help you apply what you've learned and take your growth even further.

Discover a growing collection of resources to support your journey:
- **Download Free Tools**: Access graphics, summaries, and guides to put concepts into action.
- **Try Exclusive Activities**: Dive into hands-on exercises and activities to deepen your understanding.
- **Explore Ongoing Learning**: Discover courses, webinars, workshops, and talks tailored to your needs.
- **Get Insider Insights**: Stay inspired and informed with fresh articles and ideas.
- **Stay Connected**: Join our mailing list for early access to new resources, updates, and special offers.

Be part of a community that's passionate about creating meaningful change. Start exploring today: **MagicMirrorBook.com**.

Appendix

Appendix

Mira's Social Identity Map

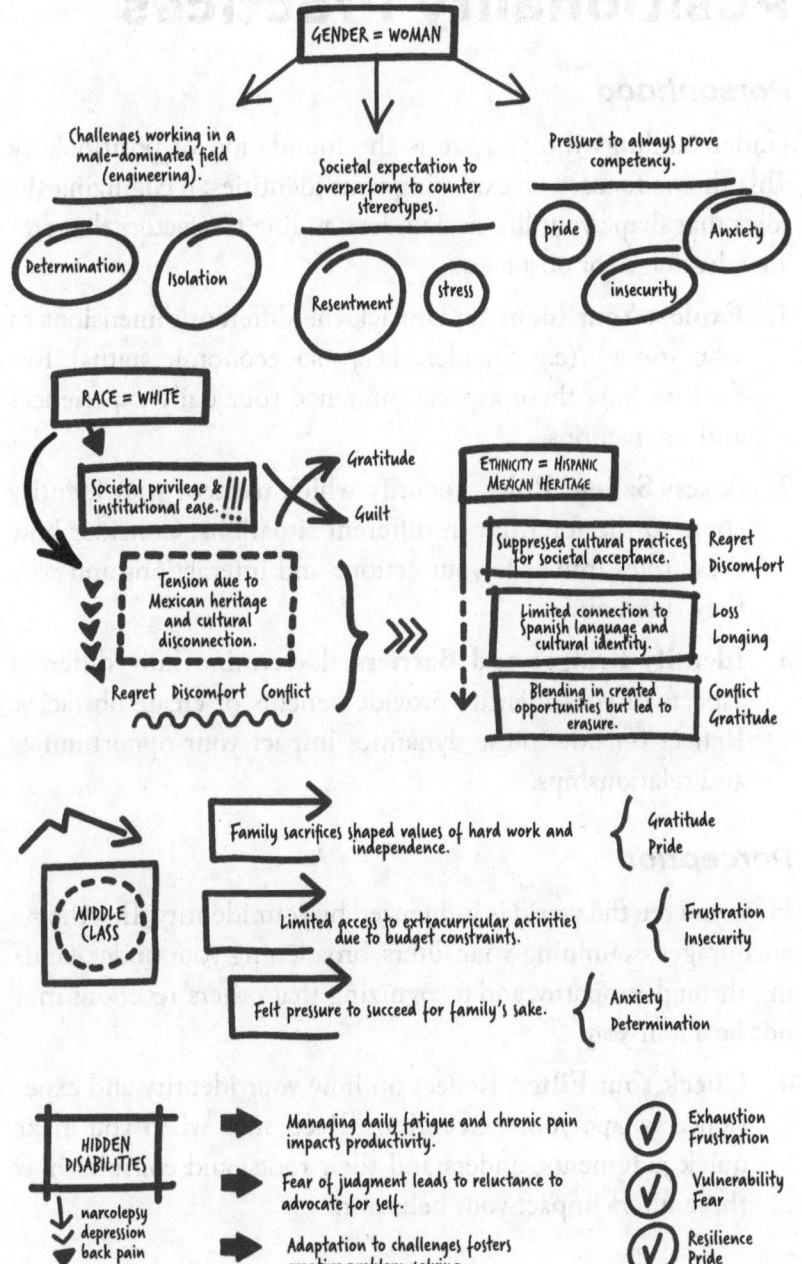

Summary of 9 Positionality Practices

Personhood

Understanding who you are is the foundation of positionality. This theme focuses on exploring your identities, recognizing the roles that shape your life, and understanding the factors that create advantages or obstacles.

1. **Explore Your Identity**: Unpack the different dimensions of who you are (e.g., gender, race, socioeconomic status). Reflect on how these aspects influence your daily experiences and interactions.
2. **Assess Salient Roles**: Identify which parts of your identity come to the forefront in different situations. Consider how these roles influence your actions and interactions and why they stand out.
3. **Identify Bridges and Barriers**: Determine how different aspects of your identity provide benefits or create obstacles. Reflect on how these dynamics impact your opportunities and relationships.

Perception

How you see the world is influenced by your identity. This theme encourages examining your filters, broadening your understanding through empathy, and recognizing that others' reactions may not be about you.

4. **Check Your Filter**: Reflect on how your identity and experiences shape your perceptions. Recognize when you make quick judgments, understand their roots, and consider how these filters impact your behavior.

5. **Expand Your Perspective**: Challenge your initial assumptions by engaging in perspective-taking. Lean into empathy by asking, "What else might be true?" to better understand others' actions and motivations.

6. **See Beyond Yourself**: Understand that others' reactions are often shaped by their own experiences and struggles. Their responses may not be about you personally—stay open and respond with empathy and respect.

Power

Power dynamics shape interactions and opportunities. This theme guides you in recognizing your own power, sharing it with others, and using it to challenge systemic barriers.

7. **Recognize Your Power**: Reflect on where your power comes from—such as privilege, social connections, or access to resources. Understand how your power affects your experiences compared to others.

8. **Share Power**: Use your influence to make space for others. Ask, "Who isn't being heard?" and actively work to amplify marginalized voices.

9. **Disrupt Barriers**: Identify systemic barriers in your environment and use your power to challenge and dismantle them. Real change comes from questioning and disrupting the status quo.

SHARE YOUR STORY: Your story matters. How have these practices impacted your life? What lessons have you learned? Sharing your experiences can inspire others and shape how these ideas are understood in real life.

I'm gathering stories for a future project to highlight real-life experiences and lessons learned. Your contribution—anonymous or named—could help others on their journey and may be featured in future works, panels or discussions.

Visit **MAGICMIRRORBOOK.COM** to share your story.

Reflection and Discussion Guide

This guide is designed to support your journey through exploring themes of personhood, perception, and power. Whether reflecting individually or participating in a group discussion, these questions will help you uncover insights, consider new perspectives, and identify meaningful actions. Allow yourself time to sit with these questions, listen to others, and explore your thoughts without judgment. Growth isn't a destination—it's a process that unfolds one step at a time.

General Questions

- What was your initial impression of Mira's journey? What stood out to you most in her experiences?
- Which moments in the book felt most familiar or different from your own experiences? Why do you think that is?
- How did you feel as Mira began her exploration of her identities? Did it inspire you to think about your own identity in new ways?
- Which of the three themes or nine practices stood out to you and why?
- What small, everyday actions could you take to create a more inclusive environment in your community or workplace?
- Why is the practice of understanding positionality important, both personally and within the broader community?
- Mira's Magic Mirror Sanctuary was nestled in a forest. If you were to imagine a custom setting for the Magic Mirror designed to reflect your interests, what would it look like?

Theme 1: Personhood

- Consider your various identities, such as gender or race.

Which of these aspects of yourself feel most important to who you are? Does that change in different environments?

- How do your identities affect your day-to-day life? For instance, does one identity become more noticeable depending on where you are or who you're with?
- How would you describe your own personhood if someone asked, "Who are you, beyond your job title and relationships?"
- What did you discover when you created a social identity map? Were there any surprises?

Theme 2: Perception

- Mira practiced empathy-driven perspective-taking by asking, "What else might be true?" Reflect on a recent moment when you made a quick judgment about someone. Could there have been another story behind their actions?
- How does your life experience shape the way you see others? Can you identify a moment in the book when Mira's perception shifted and how it influenced her behavior?
- Has there ever been a time when someone misunderstood you because of how they perceived you? How did it make you feel?
- What helps you stay open to other perspectives, even when it challenges your assumptions?

Theme 3: Power

- Reflect on a time when you were in a position to make a decision that impacted others. How did you use your power in that moment?
- In what areas of your life do you notice the most barriers to sharing power with others? How can you work on breaking down those barriers?
- Mira realized that power isn't just about taking charge—it's

also about stepping back and making space for others. What does "sharing power" look like in your daily life?
- Have you ever been in a situation where you felt like your voice wasn't heard? How did it impact you? How might you create space for others to be heard?
- Can you think of any systems or practices in your workplace or community that might be limiting for some people? What small actions could you take to start challenging these limitations?

Action Commitments

- Choose one practice from the book that you feel could make a meaningful difference in your life or community. How will you apply it in the coming weeks?
- Identify one area where you could use your influence to support someone else's growth. What specific steps can you take to create that space?
- Plan to revisit these reflections in a few weeks. What progress do you notice, and what new challenges have arisen?

Visit MagicMirrorBook.com to **DOWNLOAD THIS GUIDE** and also access expanded versions customized for various audiences. You are also invited to submit prompt suggestions!

Key Terms

Language is constantly evolving, reflecting shifts in our understanding of ourselves and the world around us. The definitions provided in this glossary are meant as a current resource for your journey, recognizing that words have power—power to perpetuate harm or foster change. *These definitions offer a foundation for understanding, but it is important to remember that they will change over time, just as our perspectives grow and evolve.*

Ableism: The system of oppression based on ability; assumes disabled people are flawed, insufficient, and inferior, resulting in the marginalization of people with disabilities. It is characterized by the unearned privilege afforded to non-disabled individuals.

Ally and Allyship: An ally is someone who actively supports and advocates for the rights and well-being of marginalized groups. Allyship is the active and consistent practice of using one's privilege to listen, learn, and take concrete steps to challenge injustice. Effective allyship requires humility, self-awareness, and a commitment to fostering equity by amplifying marginalized voices and working to dismantle systemic barriers.

Asset Mindset: An approach to problem-solving, learning, and collaboration that emphasizes strengths, resources, and potential rather than focusing solely on deficits or challenges. It encourages recognizing and respectfully valuing different ways of knowing, doing, and being, as contributions, or assets, to a team or environment.

Belonging: A sense of security and support where individuals feel accepted, included, and valued for who they are within a group or community. Belonging goes beyond inclusion by fostering meaningful connections and allowing individuals to bring their authentic selves to the environment.

Bias: A tendency to favor or lean toward a particular perspective, often unconsciously. Biases can be positive or negative and influence decisions, perceptions, and actions toward others. **Implicit bias** refers to the attitudes or stereotypes that affect one's understanding, actions, and decisions in an unconscious manner.

Biological Sex: A classification based on physical and physiological characteristics such as chromosomes, hormones, and reproductive anatomy. Commonly categorized as male, female, or intersex, though it is distinct from gender identity.

Bro Culture: A social or workplace environment dominated by hyper-masculine behaviors, often marginalizing those who do not conform to traditional male norms. Bro culture can perpetuate stereotypes, discourage diversity, and create an unwelcoming environment for women and marginalized groups.

Calling Out vs. Calling In: There are two approaches to addressing harmful behavior or language. Calling In is a more effective approach that involves conversation, compassion, and context. It invites people into the conversation with respect and fosters education and growth. While it does not have to be private, it emphasizes collaboration and respect. Calling Out, by contrast, assumes the worst and publicly addresses behavior to hold individuals accountable. It is often used when the harm is severe or prior efforts have failed.

Cisgender: A person whose sense of personal identity and gender expression corresponds with their birth sex. For example, a person assigned male at birth who identifies as a man and presents their gender in ways typically associated with masculinity.

Confirmation Bias: The tendency to search for, interpret, and remember information that confirms one's pre-existing beliefs or biases while disregarding information that contradicts those beliefs.

Cultural Capital and Wealth: The accumulation of knowledge, behaviors, skills, and resources (such as education, intellect, style of speech, and style of dress) that promote social mobility within a stratified society. Cultural wealth extends this concept to include the strengths and assets of marginalized communities, such as familial networks, resilience, and community knowledge, highlighting how these contribute to navigating and thriving within systems of inequality.

Key Terms

Culture: The shared beliefs, values, norms, customs, behaviors, and artifacts that characterize a group or society. Culture shapes the way individuals perceive and interact with the world.

Deficit Mindset: A perspective that focuses on perceived weaknesses, shortcomings, or failures within individuals, groups, or systems rather than recognizing and building upon their strengths, potential, or resources. This mindset often leads to negative assumptions, low expectations, and limited opportunities for growth or success. Opposite of an asset mindset.

Dehumanization: The process of depriving a person or group of people of their humanity, treating them as less than human, often through language, actions, or policies. This can manifest in stereotyping, objectification, or systemic oppression, and is frequently used to justify discrimination, violence, or exclusion.

Disability: Any condition of the body or mind (impairment) that makes it more difficult for the person with the condition to do certain activities (activity limitation) and interact with the world around them (participation restrictions).

Discrimination: The unjust or prejudicial treatment of individuals or groups based on characteristics such as race, gender, age, religion, disability, or socioeconomic status.

Dominant Group or Dominant Culture: The group that holds the most power in a given society sets norms, values, and expectations that are considered standard. Subordinate groups, also called target groups, lack power and are often marginalized or excluded from shaping the cultural narrative or accessing resources.

Equity: The fair treatment, access, opportunity, and advancement for all people while striving to identify and eliminate barriers that have prevented the full participation of some groups. Equity is different from equality in that it acknowledges that different people have different needs.

Equality: The state of being equal, especially in status, rights, and opportunities. Unlike equity, equality implies that everyone receives the same resources or opportunities regardless of differing needs.

Ethnicity: A social construct that divides people into smaller social groups based on characteristics such as a shared sense of group membership, values, behavioral patterns, language, political and economic interests, history, and ancestral geographical base.

Food Desert and Food Mirage: A food desert refers to an area where access to affordable, nutritious food is limited or nonexistent, often due to a lack of grocery stores or fresh food markets. Conversely, a food mirage describes an area where healthy food options appear to be available but are economically inaccessible to the community, such as stores with overpriced goods relative to the local income levels.

Fundamental Attribution Error: The tendency to overemphasize personal characteristics and ignore situational factors when explaining someone else's behavior. It leads to assumptions that people's actions are based on their nature rather than external influences.

Gender: A socially constructed system of classification that ascribes qualities of masculinity and femininity to people. Gender is typically assigned at birth based on biological sex and may or may not align with an individual's internal sense of identity.

Gender Expression/Image/Display: The external presentation of oneself as gendered through cultural identifiers and markers such as clothing, behaviors, etc.

Gender Identity: A person's internal sense of themselves as a specific gender. Gender identity may not always match gender expression.

Genderqueer: A self-identifying term for someone who rejects the male/female gender binary in favor of a more fluid, nontraditional identity that merges or blurs characteristics of gender and gender norms.

Heterosexism: The system of oppression that assumes heterosexuality as the norm, favors heterosexuals, and denigrates and stigmatizes anyone whose gender or sexual behavior is considered non-heterosexual. Heterosexism is closely tied to rigid gender norms, as it reinforces binary gender roles and expectations that align with heterosexuality while marginalizing those who do not conform to these norms.

Ideology: A system of ideas and ideals that form the basis of economic or political theories and policies, as well as social norms. Ideologies can influence how people perceive and treat others and often form the foundation of systemic oppression.

Imposter Syndrome: A form of internalized oppression where individuals feel they are not deserving of their accomplishments, despite evidence of their competence. Imposter syndrome is not a personal flaw or a badge to wear; it is a result of external systemic pressures that lead people, particularly those from marginalized groups (individuals or groups pushed to the edge of society through lack of access to rights, resources, and opportunities), to question and doubt their value. Read the Harvard Business Review article by Ruchika Tulshyan and Jodi-Ann Burey, Stop Telling Women They Have Imposter Syndrome.

Inclusion: The practice of creating environments where all individuals feel valued, respected, and have access to the same opportunities, regardless of their identities or backgrounds.

Institutional Oppression: The policies, practices, and procedures within and across institutions (such as education, law, healthcare, and employment) that systematically disadvantage certain groups while benefiting others. Institutional oppression is a part of broader systemic inequality.

Internalized Oppression: The process by which members of marginalized or minoritized groups come to believe and accept negative stereotypes, ideologies, and stigmas about themselves. It leads to self-limiting beliefs and behaviors that conform to these oppressive norms.

Interlocking 4-I Model: A model used to describe how oppression operates at four interlocking levels: Ideological, Interpersonal, Institutional, and Internalized. These levels interact and reinforce each other to perpetuate systems of inequity and injustice. Learn more at https://drmp.co/4i

Interpersonal Oppression: Interpersonal oppression refers to the ways discrimination and prejudice are enacted between individuals. This includes conscious and unconscious biases that manifest in behaviors such as stereotyping, microaggressions, exclusion, or overt acts of racism and sexism. These interactions reinforce systemic inequities on a personal level.

Intersectionality: Intersectionality is a framework developed by Kimberlé Crenshaw that examines how various social identities (such as race, gender, class, and sexuality) intersect to create overlapping systems of oppression or privilege. It helps to understand the unique experiences of individuals affected by multiple forms of discrimination.

LGBT, LGBTQ+, LGBTQIA: Umbrella terms used to refer to the community as a whole. The letters stand for Lesbian, Gay, Bisexual, Transgender, Queer, Questioning, Intersex, Asexual, and Allied.

Marginalized: Groups or individuals pushed to the edge of society through lack of access to rights, resources, and opportunities. Marginalization often results from systemic discrimination and unequal power dynamics.

Meritocracy: A system or belief that success and opportunities are based solely on individual talent, effort, and achievement, often overlooking systemic barriers and privileges that influence access to resources and outcomes.

Microaggressions: Subtle, often unintentional, behaviors or comments that convey negative or derogatory messages about a marginalized group, perpetuating stereotypes and systemic inequalities.

Microassaults: Explicit, deliberate actions or statements meant to cause harm or express bias against a marginalized group. Examples include racial slurs, discriminatory gestures, or overt exclusion.

Microinequities: Small, often unnoticed actions or behaviors that signal devaluation, exclusion, or bias toward someone based on their identity. These can accumulate over time to create a culture of inequity.

Minoritized: The process of being treated as a minority or being socially, economically, and politically positioned as "less than." This term emphasizes that being a minority is not about numerical status but is about how power structures actively position groups as inferior.

Nationality: The legal relationship between an individual and a specific nation-state, often granting rights such as citizenship, protection, and responsibilities. Nationality can be based on place of birth, naturalization, or descent.

Neurodivergent: A term used to describe individuals whose neurological development and functioning differ from what is considered typical or normative. It includes conditions like autism, ADHD, dyslexia, and other cognitive differences.

Oppression: The systematic and pervasive mistreatment of individuals based on their membership in a marginalized group. It involves both formal structures (such as laws and policies) and informal social norms that reinforce inequality and disadvantage.

Personhood: Refers to the intrinsic value and dignity of an individual as a unique and autonomous being. It emphasizes recognizing oneself and others as fully human, with rights, agency, and the capacity for growth.

Perception: The process through which individuals interpret and make sense of their experiences and the world around them. Perception is influenced by positionality, including social identities, lived experiences, and biases, shaping how one sees and interacts with others.

Positionality: The social and political context that creates your identity and influences and biases your perception of and outlook on the world.

Positionality Prism: A framework that views positionality as a prism through which individuals perceive and interpret the world, shaped by intersecting aspects of identity such as race, gender, class, and ability. This concept emphasizes that positionality affects both how individuals experience power and privilege and how they contribute to systemic inequities or change. By understanding the layers of their positionality, individuals can recognize biases, challenge assumptions, and act more equitably.

Power: The ability to influence outcomes, control resources, and shape decisions. Power is not always formal; it can be found in relationships, social connections, knowledge, and privilege. Within the Positionality Prism framework, power is understood as shaped by intersecting aspects of identity such as race, gender, and class, highlighting its dynamic and context-dependent nature.

Prejudice: Prejudice is a preconceived opinion that is not based on reason or actual experience.

Privilege: A special right, advantage, or immunity granted or available only to a particular person or group. It involves unearned benefits that are given to individuals because of their membership in dominant social groups.

Psychological Safety: A shared belief within a group or team that it is safe to take interpersonal risks, express ideas, ask questions, or admit mistakes without fear of embarrassment, rejection, or punishment. This environment fosters trust, collaboration, and innovation by valuing respect and mutual support.

Queer: A reclaimed term used by some LGBTQ+ people to describe diverse sexual orientations, gender identities, or a sense of community. While inclusive and empowering for many, its historical use as a slur means it should be used respectfully and typically for self-identification.

Race: A social construct that divides people into groups based on physical appearance, ancestry, culture, history, etc. Notions of racial difference are human creations rather than biological categories and have evolved over history.

Racism: A system of oppression based on the belief that one race is superior to others. It manifests through individual, interpersonal, institutional, and systemic actions and policies that discriminate against and marginalize people based on race. Racism is maintained by power structures and social norms that reinforce racial hierarchies and inequities.

Salient Identities: The aspects of a person's identity that are most prominent in a particular context. Salient identities can change depending on the environment or the situation, affecting how a person feels and how they are perceived by others.

Self-Determination: The ability or process by which a person controls their own life, sets goals, and makes decisions free from external influence or coercion.

Self-Efficacy: The belief in one's ability to succeed in specific situations or accomplish a task. Self-efficacy plays an essential role in how goals, tasks, and challenges are approached.

Self-Regulation: Self-regulation is the ability to manage one's behaviors, including the ability to set specific goals, and to use appropriate strategies to attain those goals. It is the process of acting in an intentional manner, often through mechanisms of cognitive control.

Sexism: A system of oppression and discrimination based on gender, typically favoring men and enforcing gender roles that marginalize women, nonbinary individuals, and others who do not conform to traditional norms. Sexism manifests through interpersonal interactions, institutional practices, cultural norms, and systemic inequalities.

Social Capital: The networks of relationships among people who live and work in a particular society, enabling that society to function effectively.

Social Class: Refers to a person's socioeconomic status based on factors such as wealth, occupation, education, income, etc.

Social Construct: An idea that has been created and accepted by the people in a society.

Social Identity Map: A visual tool used to explore and reflect on various aspects of one's identity (such as race, gender, religion, ability, etc.). This helps to understand how different elements of identity intersect and influence one's experiences, opportunities, and challenges.

Socioeconomic Status (SES): A measure of an individual or family's economic and social position relative to others, based on income, education, and occupation. Often synonymous with "class," SES highlights disparities in access to resources and opportunities.

Stereotypes: Widely held but fixed, oversimplified, and generalized images or ideas of a particular type of person or thing, including personal traits or circumstantial attributes. Stereotypes can become ideological beliefs that lead to assumptions about characteristics, behaviors, and social norms.

Stereotype Threat: The risk of confirming a negative stereotype about one's group, which can lead to increased anxiety and decreased performance in certain situations.

STEM: An acronym for Science, Technology, Engineering, and Mathematics. STEM fields are often associated with innovation and economic growth, and increasing diversity within these fields is a key focus for promoting broader social equity.

Systemic Oppression: A form of oppression that encompasses various -isms, such as racism, sexism, classism, and ableism. These -isms manifest across four interlocking levels: Ideological, Interpersonal, Institutional, and Internalized. Systemic oppression is entrenched in the laws, policies, and practices of societal institutions, perpetuating inequality and keeping certain groups at a disadvantage.

Tokenize: To treat an individual from a marginalized group as a symbolic representative of their group, often for appearances of diversity or inclusion, rather than valuing their unique contributions or perspectives. Tokenization can perpetuate stereotypes and reinforce inequities.

Toxic Positivity: The excessive or insincere promotion of a happy or optimistic attitude, regardless of circumstances. It dismisses or invalidates authentic emotions and struggles, creating an environment where individuals feel pressured to suppress negative feelings.

Transgender: An umbrella term for people whose gender identity and/or expression is different from cultural expectations based on the sex they were assigned at birth. Transgender people may identify as straight, gay, lesbian, bisexual, etc.

Key Terms 199

White Fragility: A term coined by Dr. Robin DiAngelo describing the defensiveness, discomfort, or guilt that many white people exhibit when confronted with discussions about racism, privilege, or inequality. This reaction often hinders meaningful dialogue and perpetuates systemic inequities.

White Women's Tears: A term referring to the emotional distress white women may display in response to being confronted about their role in systemic racism or interpersonal harm. This behavior can shift focus away from accountability and toward their own feelings, often perpetuating harm to marginalized individuals.

Xenophobia: Fear, hatred, or prejudice against people from other countries or cultures, often manifesting as discrimination, exclusion, or hostility toward immigrants or those perceived as foreign.

Endnotes & Additional Reading

Over the past 15 years, I've explored countless articles, papers, and books that inform the Positionality Prism and the 9 Practices. This book, however, is intentionally not an academic text. Rather than overwhelming readers with research, I chose to focus on storytelling to make these ideas accessible and engaging. What follows is a selection of additional readings on positionality—some of which are works I frequently reference, though this list is far from exhaustive. It also includes the few endnotes referenced in this text, along with other resources cited for those who wish to explore further.

Positionality

- Hampton, C., & Reeping, D. (2019). *Positionality: The stories of self that impact others*. Paper presented at the 2019 ASEE Annual Conference & Exposition, Tampa, Florida. https://doi.org/10.18260/1-2--33177
- Holmes, A. G. D. (2020). Researcher positionality: A consideration of its influence and place in qualitative research—A new researcher guide. *Shanlax International Journal of Education, 8*(4), 1–10. https://doi.org/10.34293/education.v8i4.3232
- (1) Jacobson, D., & Mustafa, N. (2019). Social identity map: A reflexivity tool for practicing explicit positionality in critical qualitative research. *International Journal of Qualitative Methods, 18*. https://doi.org/10.1177/1609406919870075
- Kassan, A., Nutter, S., Green, A. R., Arthur, N., Russell-Mayhew, S., & Sesma-Vasquez, M. (2020). Capturing the Shadow and Light of Researcher Positionality: A Picture-Prompted Poly-Ethnography. *International Journal of Qualitative Methods*, 19. https://doi.org/10.11575/PRISM/46476
- Martin, J. P., Desing, R., & Borrego, M. (2022). Positionality statements are just the tip of the iceberg: Moving towards a reflexive process. *Journal of Women and Minorities in Science and*

- *Engineering, 28*(4), v–vii. https://doi.org/10.1615/JWomenMinorScienEng.2022044277
- Mercer, L. E., & Moses, T. (2023). Positionality. In *Racism untaught: Revealing and unlearning racialized design* (pp. 95–132). The MIT Press. https://doi.org/10.7551/mitpress/15077.001.0001
- Secules, S., McCall, C., Mejia, J. A., Beebe, C., Masters, A., Sánchez-Peña, M. L., & Svyantek, M. (2021). Positionality practices and dimensions of impact on equity research: A collaborative inquiry and call to the community. *Journal of Engineering Education, 110*(1), 19–43. https://doi.org/10.1002/jee.20377

Other Resources Mentioned In the Text

- (2) National Center for Science and Engineering Statistics, National Survey of College Graduates, 2021. Employed scientists and engineers, by occupation, highest degree level, and sex. https://ncses.nsf.gov/pubs/nsf23315/table/1-2
- (3) McIntosh, P. (1989). White privilege: Unpacking the invisible knapsack. Peace and Freedom Magazine, July/August, 1989, pp. 10-12, a publication of the Women's International League for Peace and Freedom, Philadelphia, PA. https://drmp.co/mcintosh
- (4) Interlocking 4-I Model was inspired by John Bell's writing, The four "I's" of oppression (https://www.joliet86.org/assets/1/6/Four_Is_of_Oppression.pdf) and The 1977 Combahee River Collective Statement (https://www.blackpast.org/african-american-history/combahee-river-collective-statement-1977/).
- Crenshaw, K. (2016, October). The urgency of intersectionality [TEDWomen Talk]. TED. https://www.ted.com/talks/kimberle_crenshaw_the_urgency_of_intersectionality
- Pipes, E. (2016, July 29). *Legos and the 4 I's of oppression* [Video]. YouTube. https://youtu.be/3WWyVRo4Uas
- Yosso, T. J. (2005). Whose culture has capital? A critical race theory discussion of community cultural wealth. *Race Ethnicity and Education, 8*(1), 69–91. https://doi.org/10.1080/1361332052000341006

Visit MagicMirrorBook.com for More Articles and Tools

Acknowledgments

Creating *Magic Mirror* has been a journey of reflection, learning, and growth, and I owe a heartfelt thanks to the many remarkable individuals who have supported and inspired this work. Your insights, feedback, and encouragement have been instrumental in bringing this project to life.

Colleagues and Mentors

Throughout my journey, I've been fortunate to have both formal professors and informal guides, like Elara, who have shaped my understanding of the world. Their lessons and insights mirror many of the challenges and revelations explored in Mira's story, and their influence is woven throughout this book.

- Dr. Donna Enerson introduced me to privilege by reading Dr. Peggy McIntosh's "Unpacking the Invisible Knapsack" in her qualitative research class.
- Dr. Brenda Capobianco taught me that gender and race are social constructs (ideas created and accepted by the people in a society).
- Dr. Lisa Williams encouraged me to consider systems in my work, a perspective that took me time to fully appreciate.
- Dr. Kacey Beddoes and Dr. Alice Pawley deepened my understanding of intersectionality, helping me see how my experiences intersect with broader social systems.
- Dr. Alisha Sarang-Sieminski introduced me to the 4-I's of oppression, exemplified by Eliana Pipes' Lego stop motion YouTube video, which profoundly shaped my thinking.
- Dr. Kelly Cross, Dr. Liz Litler, and Dr. Linda Vanasupa provided critical insights into understanding white supremacy.
- Dr. Chanel Beebe, Dr. James Holly Jr., Dr. Kayla Maxey, Dr. Brooke Coley, and others helped me explore anti-racism in engineering.

- Finally, Tegwin Pulley, my mentor since I was 18 and an intern at Texas Instruments, has been a steadfast champion and cheerleader. Her "What else might be true?" prompt continues to guide me and remains one of the most valuable tools I've learned and shared in this book.

Clients and Supporters

This book was inspired by my original 26-page positionality worksheet, the most downloaded resource on my company website. To everyone who used this tool and shared reflections—your contributions refined and expanded its impact, shaping the foundation of this book.

Thank you to my clients and everyone who has engaged with my services and broader body of work, downloaded free resources, or joined the mailing list. The greatest compliment I can receive is when people use my services and resources to advance social awareness and inclusion. I hope this book serves as a valuable tool for your journey toward greater social consciousness. If you're not yet on the list, join at https://engineerinclusion.com/list/. Perhaps one of the next tools I share with my list will inspire you, too. Who knows which tool will inspire the next book?

Early Readers

This book would not be the same without my early readers' thoughtful and constructive feedback. To read a book and offer critical feedback takes time, energy, and heart—and to do so within 11 days is nothing short of remarkable. Each of these people invested in this book's potential because they believe in the work, and for that, I am incredibly grateful. Your insights and encouragement made all the difference:

- **Lauren Jones**: Your push to include more of Mira's struggles added depth and realism to her story, balancing optimism with authenticity. Thank you for encouraging me to humanize her journey in a way that resonates with readers. You also inspired many of the graphics and imagery.

- **Natalie Hernandez**: Your detail-oriented feedback and cultural insights sharpened the manuscript's authenticity. Your suggestions helped refine contradictions and elevate representation, ensuring the story connects with diverse audiences.

- **Andrea Ragonese**: Your love for descriptive writing inspired me to lean into the vivid imagery that gives *Magic Mirror* its magic. Your keen editorial eye polished the manuscript beautifully.

- **Kelsey Peterson**: Your valuable suggestions and perspectives offered clarity and real-world insight, particularly as someone navigating the challenges of this work. Thank you for helping me fine-tune the rhythm and practical relevance of this story.

- **Jennifer Hiltebeitel**: Thank you for helping me remove overused adjectives. Your feedback was as "gentle and warm" as the edits you inspired! Catching key narrative inconsistencies improved clarity and coherence.

- **Iris Yong**: Your perspective expanded the manuscript's inclusivity, and challenged some U.S.-centric language. You also caught a critical thread I had forgotten to pick back up in Mira and Ruby's story, ensuring the narrative remained cohesive and impactful.

Tools

Writing this book during a challenging time in my life brought light and purpose. Inspired by National Novel Writing Month (#NaNoWriMo), I started manifesting the concept and writing on November 4, 2024, and sent a draft to early readers by December 4. Tools like ChatGPT and Grammarly assisted with brainstorming, accessibility, and editing, but the work remains entirely my own. The mirror on the cover was imagined with MidJourney, and I handled all graphic design and layout work.

Personal Thanks

- To my parents, Phil and DeAnne: I am deeply grateful for the foundation you provided and for your encouragement to strive for excellence. In many ways, this book reflects my hope that you might better understand why this work matters so much to me. Your influence has shaped my perseverance and drive, even as I navigate my unique path.

- To Jaz, the foster child who lived with me during this time and who I had hoped to adopt: While your journey has taken a different direction, your presence during those months left an enduring imprint on my heart. I wish you nothing but hope and happiness as you pursue your future.

- To Molly, my loyal blue nose pitbull: Your companionship during long writing sessions—complete with toy-fetching and cuddle breaks—kept me grounded and joyful. I hope readers enjoyed her cameos in the book.

Finally, to you, the readers who have chosen to walk alongside Mira on this journey, thank you from the bottom of my heart. Your willingness to engage with her story and share this book with others means the world to me. Together, we can inspire new perspectives and create ripples of understanding and inclusion. Thank you for your belief in the power of this story to inspire change.

ABOUT THE AUTHOR

DR. MEAGAN POLLOCK began her career as an engineer at Texas Instruments, working with microscopic mirrors to project light with precision. Today, she uses metaphorical projectors and mirrors to illuminate and adjust the social systems that shape our lives. Through her company, Engineered Organizations, Meagan helps leaders design intentional strategies that improve collaboration, innovation, and success across teams and organizations.

A TEDx speaker on leadership and culture, author of the modern fable MAGIC MIRROR, and former National Science Foundation Graduate Research Fellow, Meagan holds a PhD in Engineering Education from Purdue University, an MS in Electrical Engineering from Texas Tech University, and a BS in Computer Science from Texas Woman's University.

As an engineer turned educator, Meagan empowers individuals and organizations to intentionally design cultures where people and progress thrive.

Learn more about Meagan's work or invite her to speak at **engineeredorgs.com**.

www.ingramcontent.com/pod-product-compliance
Lightning Source LLC
Chambersburg PA
CBHW011521070526
44585CB00022B/2497